CW00407583

HOW TO
BE A HERO

LT. O'HARE

HOW TO BE A HERO

SAM MARTIN

APPLE

First published in the UK in 2008 by
Apple Press
7 Greenland Street
London
NW1 0ND
www.apple-press.com

Conceived and produced by
Elwin Street Limited
144 Liverpool Road
London N1 1LA
www.elwinstreet.com

ISBN 978-1-84543-248-5

Designed by Jon Wainwright, Alchemedia Design
Illustrations by David Eaton
Picture credits: Corbis – 8, Getty Images – 12, 24, 26, 33, 39, 44,
48, 53, 57, 64, 69, 76, 80, 86, 93, 94, 98, 108, 110, 117.

10 9 8 7 6 5 4 3 2 1

Printed in Singapore

CONTENTS

INTRODUCTION

In January 2007, a 50-year-old construction worker in New York City named Wesley Autrey jumped onto subway tracks to save a 20-year-old student who had fallen off the platform while having a seizure. With the Number 1 train fast approaching, Autrey grabbed the man, pulled him into the middle of the tracks and laid on top of him while the train rolled over them. When the train stopped, both men crawled out from under it. The student was unharmed. Autrey was an instant hero.

Would you do that? That's a tough one to answer because if you have to stop and think about it, you've already got it wrong. In other words, I'm not sure Autrey, the Subway Hero, thought too much before he acted. He saw someone in danger and he saved them – that's what heroes do. They are experts at not thinking.

Now that's not to say heroes are dumb – being ready to act on instinct doesn't mean you're stupid. On the contrary, they're usually very well-prepared. Luck might have something to do with it, but as the saying goes, luck comes to the well-prepared.

My guess is that Autrey was an avid subway rider. In fact, he must have ridden the subway every day, at least twice a day, for years, perhaps decades, before he saved that student's life. While he was waiting for trains all those years, it's quite possible he imagined someone falling onto the tracks and he imagined what he would do if he had to jump after them. Maybe he saw the trough between the tracks and, being a construction worker, estimated it fairly accurately, deciding a man could probably fit in there unharmed while a train rolled overhead.

What I'm suggesting is that, in some way, whether he knew it or not, Autrey was prepared for the emergency and the actions he took. He may not have gone through any subway track rescue drills, and yes, it still took courage and confidence to jump down there – you'll know how much if you've ever seen the filthy, rat-infested New York subways – but the bottom line is that Autrey was prepared. He knew what he had to do and he did it.

So for all you burgeoning heroes out there, who think you have that can-do attitude in you but need an extra boost to prepare yourself for a real emergency, this book is for you. With the know-how in these pages, you can learn how to act or react in an emergency, or any dire situation that might call for a hero. You can learn about the many types of heroes out there, and pick a role model for your own heroics. Sometimes a hero has to save himself before he can save others, so there's a whole chapter on personal survival skills. And of course, one of the most heroic jobs any man can do is romance and care for the women in his life, so no book on heroism would be complete without a chapter on the fairer sex. The concept of chivalry takes on a whole new meaning in the life of a hero.

As you read through the book consider that maybe the real difference between a hero and everyone else is the 'doing it' part. We can all learn how to save someone from a burning building, treat a gunshot wound, survive in the great outdoors or dance the tango, but courage and the willingness to put yourself at risk for the well-being of others can't be taught. That's something you have to learn on the job.

And lastly, don't think that being a hero means giving up the day job to patrol the streets looking for trouble. Heroes are needed everyday and everywhere, whether they're picking their kids up from school, bringing home a salary from work, cooking dinner for their sweethearts or chasing down a mugger. The first task for any hero is taking a deliberate step into the game of life. Once you're there, play your heart out.

CHAPTER

1

PLAYING THE PART

One question I get all the time is, 'If you want to be a hero do you have to wrestle an alligator?' While that might help (assuming you come out on top), it's not necessary. In fact, most heroic acts might seem mundane; helping a lady cross the road or rescuing the neighbour's cat from a tree are acts of heroism in their own ways. The best way to become the hero you want to be is to just be yourself. If you don't know who you are, the following pages contain a few different types of men to help you uncover the hero within.

LOOKING HEROIC

Heroes come in all types, sizes, shapes and colours so unless you prefer to wear a cape and a wide gold belt there is no one uniform or look (or hero). In fact, most of the time we heroes don't have time to dash into a phone box to change clothes. We have to act with what we have on, whether it be a towel or a tie. That said, there's nothing wrong with taking notice of a few basics. If you really need to go the superhero route, get to the fabric store and find yourself a good sewing machine. After that you're on your own.

What to wear

1. Sturdy boots and/or shoes. This is perhaps the only real piece of equipment that will make a difference to whether you can run down the pickpocket or whisk a young boy out of the way of oncoming traffic, or not.

2. Jeans. Jeans are cotton so they won't catch fire easily if you have to rush into a burning building or you find yourself in a plane crash. Plus, you're less likely to get mugged on a dark street wearing these than your white linen suit.

3. Stylish shirts and jackets. During emergencies and disasters you want to be in charge and people will take you more seriously if you're dressed nicely – as if you really are in charge.

4. Sunglasses. These help if you get held up at gunpoint, as shading your eyes will help retain the element of surprise. Or if you're forced to patrol a sunny beach to ensure the safety of many dozens of bikini-clad women.

5. Watch. You'll need to synchronise with other agents, keep tabs on how much time is left before the bomb goes off, and be on time to your girlfriend's birthday dinner.

THE RIGHT EXPRESSIONS AND STANCES

Once you get your clothing basics all sorted out, it's time to work on your facial expressions and body language. Yes, it does make a difference. There are times when nothing else will work except a good scowl or a snarl, especially if you're trying to intimidate any would be muggers or assailants. Practice yours in the mirror to make sure you look convincing and that you won't be inviting a punch rather than scaring one off.

If you're asking a girl to dance or saving Grandma's cat from a tree, loose the scowl. No one likes a hero with a bad attitude. When you're trying to help people out, you want to put them at their ease and usually calm them down, so a reassuring smile is the best facial expression to adopt. Smiles will always win supporters, relieve tension and sometimes even unnerve bank robbers.

When it comes to the right stance, you want to look impressive, confident and in control. Anytime you're confronted with danger, spread your legs slightly apart and balance your weight on both feet. Centre your gravity and get ready to pounce.

You may find that you are always confronted with danger and wish to stand with your legs slightly apart no matter what the occasion. Feel free. Try placing your hands on your waist as you do this to get an even greater superhero effect.

ROLES TO AVOID

Just as Luke Skywalker chose the Jedi and Darth Vader opted for the dark side, there are diverging paths in the world of heroes. All are available to those just getting started so you want to weigh your options carefully, choose well and then try to stick to your path. What you don't want to do is start out a hero then make some mistakes and end up dead or get too cynical from an oversized ego combined with a lack of perceived respect and turn to the dark side of villainy. Statistics show that the good guys win more often that not.

QUALITIES OF A HERO

You don't have to be Mr Universe to perform heroic acts. Heroes come in all shapes and sizes, and no matter what type of man you think you are, there's a good chance you have some of the qualities of a hero. These qualities haven't changed much over the years and are good characteristics to strive for regardless of whether you're aspiring to heroic status or not. If you don't have any of these qualities, never fear. They can be learned.

Heroic qualities	
Determination	Keeps a firm grasp on his intentions or actions.
Loyalty	Maintains an unyielding allegiance to a cause, action, or person.
Courage	Faces dangerous situations without fear.
Dedication	Carries a strong and constant devotion to someone or something.
Selflessness	Displays little concern for self, due to a greater concern for the good of others.
Focus	Concentrates energy on a particular purpose or goal.
Gallantry	Happily seeks adventure with great courage.
Perseverance	Maintains steadfast determination despite obstacles.
Fortitude	Remains mentally strong when enduring pain or facing adversity.
Self-sacrifice	Willing to give up things of personal value for the sake of a greater cause.

HERO ROLE MODELS

It's good to have role models, people we can look to for inspiration and an example of how to live our own heroic lives. And no matter what you do, there's always someone in that field who seems to have done the job for the right reasons and in the right way. Here are a few favourites.

Heroic role models	
Nelson Mandela	Mandela was and is a hero because he embodied a great idea: that people of all races should be free and equal under the law. Not since Abraham Lincoln has one man influenced world history so profoundly.
Oskar Schindler	Amid the hatred and madness of Europe in the Second World War, Schindler provided an example of true heroism and humanity by protecting some 1200 Jews from deportation to Nazi death camps. Sacrificing his fortune, and risking his own life many times over, he displayed true heroism in saving the lives of others no matter the cost to himself
Mohandas Gandhi	If you manage to be enough of a hero in life that you inspire other heroes then you know you've accomplished something. Gandhi did it by helping India gain its independence from the British Empire – and he did it all without violence, an example that later campaigners like Martin Luther King and Nelson Mandela were to follow.
Bill Gates	If making money is heroic, then Bill Gates, the richest man in the world, is top dog. But making the money isn't as heroic as giving it away to good causes. He and his wife have donated millions to cure malaria and fight AIDS in the world's poorest countries.

Winston Churchill	Standing tall in the face of adversity, Churchill led Europe's resistance against Nazi Germany, refusing to allow fascism to spread across the globe.
Pelé	The greatest soccer player of all time, Pelé proved that growing up in poverty is no barrier to becoming a superstar, and that no matter the colour of your skin, hard work and talent will bring you success.
Ernest Hemingway	In the literary world of the 1920s, Hemingway was a giant among men. The author helped define a generation while writing about boxers, hunters and travellers.
Sir Edmund Hillary	Physical feats of daring were for many years the trademark of the heroic set, making Hillary a hero's hero after he became the first person to reach the top of the world when he conquered Mount Everest in 1953. He was knighted soon after the climb.
Neil Armstrong	There's definitely something heroic about strapping yourself in a rocket and getting shot to the moon! Armstrong did just that and then became the first man to set foot on another world.
Muhammed Ali	Born Cassius Clay, some say Ali was the greatest boxer of all time. He was definitely the most colourful and controversial. He lost and regained the title of Heavyweight Champion three times between 1964 and 1978. He has since devoted his time and money to social causes. Ali received the American Presidential Medal of Freedom in 2005.
William Wilberforce	A member of the English Parliament in the late 18th and early 19th centuries, Wilberforce heroically spearheaded the effort to put an end to the British slave trade, providing a global example of compassion.

TYPES OF HEROES

What type of hero are you? Well, that depends on whether you lead a team at the office, like a fair bit of action or have a few young kids you take care of back home (probably the most heroic of jobs out there). Of course, those who wear a cape and have x-ray vision are in a league of their own. If this is you, skip ahead to the Emergency Rescue chapter – just leave a little glory for the rest of us.

HEAD OF THE FAMILY

It used to be that the head of the family simply meant he who brought home the bacon. Now, making money does not a hero make. Heads of families have a lot more going on these days than just filling the bank account; today, being provider means paying the bills AND playing a role in the emotional and mental well-being of other family members. That's not to say everyone is incapable of taking care of their own emotions – they just look to you for support and encouragement. The head of the house hero usually fulfils the following roles.

KEY HEROIC ATTRIBUTES

- ✓ Guardian. He's willing to protect the family's way of life and values, as well as its self-esteem and physical well-being.
- ✓ Leader. He takes the initiative on family vacations and is the first to notice and fix household problems – like a clogged toilet – as they arise, so to speak.
- ✓ Role model. Positive behaviour, encouraging words and heroic actions to be emulated by the whole family.

ROMANTIC HERO

Most heroic types, no matter which type they are, don't have any troubles getting the girl. There's something very attractive about doing good and dangerous deeds or making lots of money and then helping those in need. But getting the girl is not what being a romantic hero is all about. In fact most heroes, whether they admit it or not, are romantics at heart. They're passionate about what they do, they're sensitive to other's needs and they are one of a kind. If you ever want to work out if the hero you know is a romantic take a look to see if he has the following traits.

KEY HEROIC ATTRIBUTES

- ✓ Passion. Sometimes it's passion for a woman, more often it's for a cause. Either way it's felt so deeply that it is beyond the hero's control.
- ✓ Sensitivity. The romantic hero hides a vulnerable and gentle spirit behind a hardened outer shell and you can be sure that much pain and desire lurks beneath the surface.
- ✓ Impressiveness. We're all human, even the most heroic among us, so we're all going to have faults. But for heroes, when the going gets tough and they find themselves in need the most, they always find a way to impress.
- ✓ Individuality. Most successful men live by their own rules, rules governed by an unshakable moral code. Often, this results in early rejection by his peers and his culture.
- ✓ Inner turmoil. Because a hero plays by his own rules, he often struggles with the need to be loved and the need to be uncompromising in his quest for greatness. This can result in a melancholic nature and a moody hero.

ACTION MAN

Being an action man is no small task. You have to be willing to take the punches as well as give them. And it's not just all about brawn with the action hero. You have to have charisma too. And some skills. Otherwise, who's going to follow you out of the escape hatch and trust you to defuse the bomb? An action man needs the following to save himself and others.

KEY HEROIC ATTRIBUTES

- ✓ Charisma. Action heroes have to convince people they can be trusted with their lives.
- ✓ Fitness. You have to be physically fit and strong enough to jump into low flying helicopters and lift yourself onto fast moving trains.
- ✓ Endurance. Being able to bench press 80 kg (180 pounds) isn't going to do you any good if you have to run 40 km (25 miles).
- ✓ An adversary. All good action heroes have an evil nemesis who is both wealthy and in a position of great power. No one said being a hero was easy.
- ✓ Physical skill. You must know the correct way to land a judo chop and be agile enough on your feet to consult on multi-million dollar martial arts movies.
- ✓ Knowledge. If you want to be an action hero you have a lot of reading to do. No James Bond wannabe would parachute into hostile territory without knowing how to load and use a variety of firearms, drive a car on two wheels, jump a small canyon on a motorcycle, disarm warheads, fly planes and helicopters and disguise himself in the latest bad guy wardrobe and make-up.

CAPTAIN OF INDUSTRY

The term 'Captain of Industry' originated during the Industrial Revolution as a term for business leaders who became absurdly rich while also influencing government policy at the same time. Most of the business heroes of the past made their fortunes with a combination of business acumen, hard work, and creativity. And that's just how you can become a business hero too. There are some useful traits that all business heroes, young and old, exhibit.

KEY HEROIC ATTRIBUTES

- ✓ Leadership. Be a strong leader to inspire others to follow you towards specific goals.
- ✓ Vision. Have a strong vision so you and others know where you're leading them.
- ✓ Knowledge. Know your market. Before you can dominate a field you must thoroughly understand it.
- ✓ Innovation. Be innovative, inventive and creative. If the answers to success were obvious, everyone would be doing it already.
- ✓ Charity. Have a philanthropic vision when you do get rich so you can use your wealth to create positive change in the world.
- ✓ Dedication. A business hero is not afraid of a little hard work to ensure their success. Be prepared to put in some long office hours to get ahead in the business world. You can take time off when you make your first million.

SPORTING HERO

Sports heroes hold a special place in the world because they perform their heroics on a court or on the pitch in front of thousands. We see their triumphs as well as their failures. That said, being a true sports hero isn't just about athleticism. You can be the most athletic person in the world but if you don't understand the subtleties of the game you aren't going to win. Sports heroes have the uncanny ability to win the competition while exhibiting the drama of life in the process. They usually display the following traits.

KEY HEROIC ATTRIBUTES

- ✓ Leadership. Rarely do sports players become sports heroes without the support of their team members, but it's up to the hero to show them the way to victory by showing off the skills and the passion and then actually piling up the trophies.
- ✓ Passion. You can't win in sports without a passion for the game and sports heroes have plenty of passion to spare. These guys are known for their intensity on the field and a competitive never-say-lose attitude.
- ✓ Skill. You have to know the game to win it and sports heroes perform at a level above other players, both physically and mentally.
- ✓ Endurance. If you quit after the first failure you'll never win. Being a hero in sports is showing up year after year and leaving all you have out on the court or pitch until you win the big one.
- ✓ Sportsmanship. If you lose and your response to the opposing team is to yell profanities in a disrespectful way, you are not a sports hero. The heroes of the game shake hands and say, 'Well done, I look forward to meeting you on the pitch next year'.

INTREPID EXPLORER

The essence of exploration is the desire to experience (and maybe record) little-known places with your own eyes and perspective. The intrepid explorer hero is driven to undertake such experiences, often in the face of grave danger. Seeing as there are only a few places on this planet that haven't been seen by human eyes, the intrepid explorer will go to great lengths and take enormous risks to reach them. He'll also put life and limb at risk to try and achieved things that no other human has accomplished, like break the land speed record or circumnavigate the globe in a balloon. This type of drive comes with a particular set of features.

KEY HEROIC ATTRIBUTES

- ✓ Courage. Anyone who tries to climb Everest or aims to be the first to hang glide across the Southern Ocean has to be brave – or crazy.
- ✓ Preparedness. No expedition can work without preparation and an intrepid explorer is a master preparer who considers every option.
- ✓ Resources. These men have the contacts to access obscure countries, and the money and time to spend weeks or months out of every year getting to and returning from their destinations. They can also afford ridiculously high life insurance premiums.
- ✓ Faith. After all the preparation, intrepid heroes must have enormous amounts of faith in what they do. Without it they could not make the leap into the unknown as much as they do.

SUPERHERO

Being a Superhero requires some super-human power or ability such as having X-ray vision or knowing exactly what women want 100 per cent of the time. Those who do not have such powers can still wear the capes and suits – and be heroes – but they should be referred to as Costumed Crime-fighters. If you suspect someone does have super powers you can corroborate your opinion by checking for the following things.

KEY HEROIC ATTRIBUTES

- ☑ Super-human skills. Ability to fly, pass through walls, make oneself invisible, lift cars off the ground with one hand, shoot fire from the fingertips, etc.
- ☑ Equipment. Has really high-tech gadgets, the likes of which you've never seen. Often wears them on a utility belt.
- ☑ Disguise. Wears a mask. Wears tights and a cape, even in broad daylight.
- ☑ Seclusion. Has a 'hideout' in some out of the way place like, say, Antarctica.
- ☑ Promptness. Is never available for a beer when there is a major catastrophe somewhere in the world.

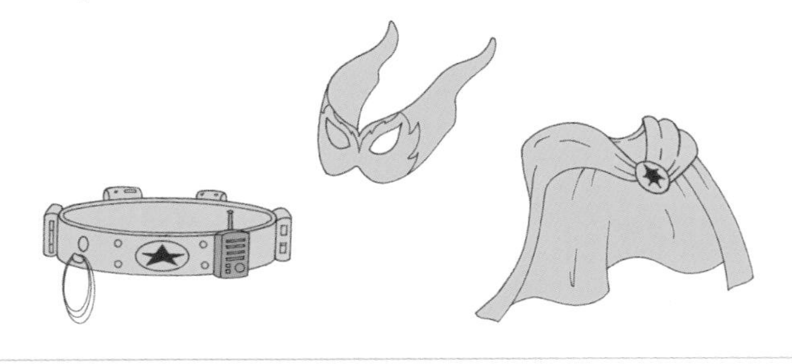

ANTI-HERO

The anti-hero is the unexpected and unconventional hero. Most people don't like him but somehow they feel for him and understand his plight. Though the anti-hero may sometimes act more like a villain, he usually possesses some decent enough intention to keep him loosely in the hero realm. The line between anti-hero and villain can get blurry. Here are some anti-hero traits.

KEY HEROIC ATTRIBUTES

- ✓ Unexceptionality. These types lack any typical heroic qualities. In fact, they're somewhat unexceptional all the way around and are more defined by how ordinary and inadequate they are.
- ✓ Confusion. These guys never know what they want. They find themselves in positions of heroism by pure chance or out of a need for self-preservation, they certainly never go looking to throw themselves into acts of heroism.
- ✓ Underhandedness. They make progress or get what they need through deceitful and cowardly means.
- ✓ Rebelliousness. The anti-hero doesn't fit into any typical mould. In fact, he actively avoids heroism out of a fear of death or damage.
- ✓ Weakness. They tend to lack the rippling muscles and firm physique of a true hero.
- ✓ Redemption. Despite all the anti-hero's faults, he somehow ends up on the right side of the law or the good side of a situation, if only just.

CHAPTER

2

HERO SKILLS

Instinct, bravery and luck go a long way in the world of heroism but so does a simple dose of know-how. Of course, heroes usually know how to do more than the average guy but unlike instinct this is not the kind of thing that you either have or you don't. There are some things you just need to know how to do, and you never know when these skills will help you save the day. It all starts with being prepared.

BEING PREPARED

It's true that some heroes are made when instinct and hidden courage reveal themselves in moments of desperation. We bow down to them. And yet, for most of us, those moments of desperation never come. Emergencies, on the other hand, come often and they can be as small as a gas leak or as large as an earthquake. Indeed, if you think about it, the chances to become a hero abound. In fact, there's an argument to be made that the most heroic among us are the most prepared. Want to be a hero? There is a list of essential items you should keep so you're always prepared for any eventuality. One is for things to keep around the house and the other is for things to put in a small bag in case you have to leave the house during an evacuation or any other emergency. You'll want to include the portable items from your first list, such as matches, batteries and a mobile phone as well. Keep these separate from the rest of your everyday goods and put the bag in a place you can grab at a moment's notice!

Home emergency kit

CHECKLIST

- ✓ A stash of torches and extra batteries
- ✓ A mobile phone AND a corded phone. Wireless phones require electricity
- ✓ Battery-powered AM/FM radio and extra batteries
- ✓ Charcoal or gas grill with extra charcoal or propane or a multi-fuel camping stove
- ✓ Canned and other foods that don't require refrigeration
- ✓ Manual can opener
- ✓ Gas or propane-powered generator
- ✓ Extra fuel
- ✓ Extra water
- ✓ Whistle to attract attention
- ✓ Matches in waterproof container
- ✓ Lighter
- ✓ Candles
- ✓ Pocket knife
- ✓ Blankets
- ✓ First aid kit
- ✓ Cooler bags in case the electricity goes out
- ✓ Propane or kerosene space heaters

continued on next page

continued

- ✓ If you have a fireplace, keep a supply of firewood around
- ✓ Battery-powered or wind-up alarm clock
- ✓ Cheques, credit cards and most importantly, cash
(Cash machines are usually down during power outages)
- ✓ Keep at least half a tank of petrol in your car at all times

HINT

✓ It's always a good idea to keep a portable emergency kit ready and to hand as well. Then if you have to leave your home in a hurry, all you have to do is grab your portable kit and go. Obviously you won't be able to take everything in your home emergency kit with you, only what you can carry. It's a good idea to include items like lightweight foods that do not require refrigeration, an extra set of car and house keys, at least five litres of water per person, a map of the area, portable toilet paper rolls or a travel pack of tissues, copies of important papers, such as personal identification and passport, and a contact information sheet with all names, addresses and phone numbers that you might need in an emergency.

FIRE-ESCAPE PLAN

A hero should do everything he can to prevent a fire but there is no planning for Uncle Fred lighting up his cigar during nap time. Now the curtains are ablaze, the fire extinguisher is empty and the light fittings are starting to melt. What you need is a fire-escape plan.

You will need

sheet of graph paper

pencil

clear plastic folder

drawing pins

HOW TO

1. To create an escape plan, draw the layout of your house, room by room, on a sheet of graph paper. Mark the locations of each window and door and label the rooms.
2. Write the word 'EXIT' in capital letters next to each door that leads to the outside.
3. Walk through the house to determine which escape routes would be the fastest in case of fire. Draw arrows on your layout of the house, showing the route each person should take to get to an exit.
4. Determine an outdoor meeting place – the neighbour's house, the corner shop – somewhere away from the fire, where you can all assemble for a head count.
5. Make sure everyone in the house knows what the plan is by walking through the escape routes and by putting the plan in a clear plastic folder and pinning it in an obvious place in the house, like near the back door or on the fridge.

DEAL WITH BURST PIPES

They might not be as serious as a severed leg artery but burst pipes still demand fast attention, so being able to deal with them is an important skill to have. Look out for them when the temperature drops below freezing, as they can crack or burst when the water inside them expands as it freezes. What you need to do is put on a temporary patch – and there are several ways to do this – and then call a plumber.

You will need

duct tape

epoxy glue or paste

pipe clamp

rubber pad

screwdriver

telephone number of a good plumber

HOW TO

1. If the crack looks small and the leak is gradual, it may be possible to wrap the pipe with duct tape without turning off the main water supply. Make sure you overlap each pass of tape as you cover the crack.
2. A more permanent patch can be made with shop-bought epoxy glue or paste, especially if the crack is near a pipe joint. Before applying any epoxy, the water must be turned off and the pipe must be thoroughly dry.
3. For a larger crack, turn the water off and place a rubber pad over the crack and around the pipe. Put half a 'C'-shaped pipe clamp over the rubber, and the other half in place so that it surrounds the rubber and the pipe, and screw them together. (If you don't have a pipe clamp, hose clamps will also work.)

4 If you've turned the water off to patch the leak, turn it back on and observe the patched section of pipe to make sure it's not leaking anymore.

HINT

✓ Prevent pipes from bursting in the first place by installing a stop and waste valve on water lines. These allow you to drain water out of pipes in anticipation of freezing temperatures. Also, you can insulate outdoor or basement pipes with foam-plastic pipe insulation or some other commercial wrapping.

CHANGE A TYRE

Getting a flat tyre in the middle of nowhere is bad. Not knowing how to change it is worse. This is one of the basics every would-be hero should know. And remember, it's not uncommon for grown men to stand on wrenches to loosen and tighten wheel nuts, so don't hesitate to do this if necessary.

You will need

flathead screwdriver

wheel wrench

jack

spare tyre

HOW TO

1. Remove spare tyre, wheel wrench, jack and screwdriver from the boot.
2. If you have a hubcap, use the screwdriver or the flat end of your wheel wrench to pry it off.
3. Use the wheel wrench to loosen the nuts on the flat tyre. Do not remove them yet. Once you've loosened the first nut, do the nut directly opposite, and continue with the others in this way.
4. Place the jack near the tyre you're changing. (Most owner's manuals show the proper placement.)
5. Jack up the car until there's enough room to remove the flat tyre and replace the spare.
6. Remove the nuts from the flat tyre and pull the tyre off.
7. Replace with spare. Lower the car, replace and tighten the wheel nuts.

DOS AND DON'TS

- ✓ Always make sure you have a properly inflated spare tyre and a working jack in your car before you set off.
- ✓ Find a safe place to pull over, and put your hazard lights on when changing a tire so that you're not putting yourself or other road users in danger.

SCORE A GOAL

There are very few things in life that can create the same sense of achievement and glory as when you see your shot hit the back of the net. For the next few minutes you feel on top of the world – you are a hero. But it does take a bit of practice, skill and sometimes, perhaps, just a little bit of luck, to score a goal. To make sure you get your time in the limelight you must take the time to practise. Time on the sports field is always fun, but if you can master the art of scoring a goal, the experience will be much more fulfilling.

WHAT TO DO

1. A scoring opportunity may arise at any moment during the game, whether through an act of brilliant skill or by blind luck. In these situations you must know when to keep the ball, and the glory, to yourself and unleash the killer shot, and when to pass it on for another player to score. When there is a gap in the defence, or the goalkeeper is out of position, shoot.

2. Create an opportunity yourself by making space around you. If defenders are too close they will hamper your movement and probably tackle you. Time a quick sprint away or perform a neat little trick when the ball comes to your feet to elude your marker.

3. You must strike the ball correctly. A toe-punt, no matter how hard or accurate, is poor technique and even if you do manage to score, no one will think you have any skill. A good striker shoots with his knee over the ball and makes contact with the laces of the boot. Always follow through in the direction you want the ball to go. This is an art, so practise.

4. You may get a chance to head the ball into the goal. The idea here is to jump up higher than the ball so that you're heading it downwards, towards the goal. Make sure you make contact with your forehead – if you use the top of your head it won't go in the right direction, and if it hits your face it will hurt. A lot.

5. Spatial awareness is key and can be learnt. In order to put the ball in the back of the net you must be able to make several calculations in a split second; how far away the goal is, the angle, the position of the opposition defenders, and where the goalkeeper is. Then you must perform your strike with the correct speed, direction and accuracy to counter the above factors.

DOS AND DON'TS

✓ Do practise your skills. There are many techniques to perfect to score a goal so learn them all well.

✗ Do not grunt loudly or scream when you hit the ball, you will sound like a female tennis player.

✗ Do not shut your eyes, flail your leg wildly or kick the ball with your toes, as you will look like an amateur and will certainly not score.

✓ Do celebrate because you deserve it! Try not to do any silly dances and thank the players who helped you (only the ones on your side, of course).

✗ Do not celebrate in an overly-elaborate fashion. People may think you've never scored a goal before. Not to mention the potential embarrassment if you manage to injure yourself through over-enthusiastic celebration moves.

KARATE KICK

There are times in every man's life when he will be called upon to defend himself or protect another. At these times of peril it is always a supreme advantage to understand some basic self-defence techniques. A well-timed and accurately-placed karate kick can immobilise an attacker and at the same time leave you ready to defend yourself again at once. It is also a lot more dignified than a bout of fisticuffs or a brutal head-butt, and if performed well should shock your attacker into instantly submitting.

You will need

baggy trousers

flexible limbs

focused ferocity

HOW TO

1. The side kick is probably the best known and coolest of the karate kicks. This is an ideal move for keeping your attacker at a safe distance and is also fairly simple to master.
2. Your target areas depend on how flexible you are as well as how close the attacker is. A good technician can aim a blow at head height, but other key areas that you could also aim for to deter your attacker are the knees, groin, stomach or solar plexus.
3. Stand side-on from your attacker with your standing leg turned 45 degrees away from them. This position will give you the base for your kick.
4. Pull your front leg up so that your knee is tucked into your body as much as

possible. Think of this as the coiled-spring moment, gathering all your energy and strength.

5. Then, with focus and ferocity, lash out at your target, keeping in mind to strike your attacker with the heel of your foot.

6. Retract your leg immediately after you have made contact and get ready to attack again, in case your assailant hasn't learnt his lesson.

DOS AND DON'TS

✓ Do stay calm; a panicky and frightened person cannot perform these moves effectively. If anxiety sets in, which it probably will, take deep breaths and clear your mind.

✗ Do not under any circumstances use a karate kick in any situation other than to defend yourself or to protect another person from attack.

RIDE A HORSE

Let's say evil aliens have landed and all the cars have stopped running. The email is down too. And so are the telephone lines. How are you going to deliver that important message? Why, on horseback, of course. Every hero has to know how to ride a horse. You just never know when you might need to.

You will need

horse

saddle

reins

sturdy bottom

HOW TO

1. If time allows, make sure your stirrups are the right length. To measure, hold onto the stirrup buckle with one hand and pull out the length of the stirrup towards your armpit with the other hand. The stirrup iron should hit your armpit exactly. If time doesn't allow for this, you're in trouble.

2. Next, put one foot in one stirrup, grab hold of the horn and pommel of the saddle (the leather part sticking up right behind the horse's neck), and swing your other leg over the back of the horse. Be sure not to kick the horse during this motion or he's liable to kick you. Either that or take off with you hanging over the side.

3. Once you're sitting in the saddle, collect the reins and make sure both feet are in the stirrups.

continued over page

continued

4. Ask the horse to go by shouting out 'yee-ha' while waving your hat in the air. Just kidding. Simply squeeze your calves slightly and the beast will begin a slow-paced walk.

5. If you would like to trot, squeeze the horse's side with your legs again. While the horse is trotting, you should rise about an inch in your saddle and then sit again, to the rhythm of the horse's gait. A trot is a two-beat gait. This is called a rising trot. Failure to rise equals a rough ride and a very sore rear end.

6. When you are ready to canter, which is faster than a trot, you should sit down and lean further back in your saddle while trotting. Then squeeze the horse again with your legs, this time slightly back a bit.

7. To slow down, sit deep (put your weight in your behind) and hold the reins.

8. To stop, squeeze the reins and sit deep; you may have to lean back a bit and put your weight into your behind and heels. Don't ever pull on the bit. Horses don't like that.

DOS AND DON'TS

✓ Always walk before trotting and trot before cantering.

✓ Whenever you stop, release the horse's reins immediately (as his reward).

✓ Always wear long trousers.

✗ Never sit or kneel near a horse.

SWIM FRONT CRAWL

When stuck out in the freezing waters of some god-forsaken sea, you will undoubtedly want to swim as quickly as possible to the nearest shore. Bear in mind that this could be a few kilometres, and at such a time, you must be able to glide smoothly and swiftly through the unforgiving seas to sanctuary and the best way to do so is with a well-executed front crawl.

You will need

ability to swim

stamina

shark repellent

HOW TO

1. Your body must be as streamlined as possible, so you should keep your head and face in the water and your entire body close to the surface.
2. Your legs should balance your body. Keep them kicking, using your whole leg. The effort should be made with the thigh for maximum thrust.
3. Your arms are your powerhouse and correct technique is vital. Raise your bent arm out of the water and over your head. Then, slice down back into the water, as far in front of you as possible. Arc your arm back toward your legs, with a slight bend in the elbow.
4. Try to breathe every two strokes, so as your arm leaves the water raise your head and look to the side, take a breath, then put your head back in the water. It is important for a good technique to breathe in time with the rhythm of the stroke.

SCALE A MOUNTAIN

When Jacques Balmat and Michel-Gabriel Paccard reached the summit of Mont Blanc in the Swiss Alps in 1786, with little more than a homemade rope tied around their waists, the heroic sport of mountain climbing was born. They were clear about the route they took to get to the top, but a bit more vague about what it took to get there. 'It was a bitch,' Balmat told his gastroenterologist some weeks after the ascent. He never elaborated.

Climbing mountains is difficult but not impossible work. You will need knowledge of rock- and snow-climbing and a good understanding of cold-weather camping and survival skills. Also, mountaineering is not a go-it-alone sport. Take at least one partner if not a group.

You will need

medium- to heavy-weight hiking boots with ankle support

two sets of warm lightweight clothing

four-season tent with guylines

warm sleeping bag

camping stove

food that is high in carbohydrates

lots of water

outdoor survival kit

HOW TO

1. Plan out your ascent and file it with the local mountain rescue force. You should plan to stop at 2400 metres (8000 feet) above sea level for at least a full day to acclimatise to the thinner air and to avoid altitude sickness. Then plan to go between 300 and 450 metres (1000 and 1500 feet) a day. Give yourself plenty of daylight time at the end of each day to set up camp for the night.

2. Start your hike slowly and go at your own pace. If fellow climbers pass you on the way, let them. This is not a race to the top. However, don't fall so far behind that you find yourself all alone. If you're

climbing rope

harness

crampons

ice axe

climbing with a large group there should be a well-trained professional bringing up the rear anyway. He shouldn't leave you behind.

3. When you get above 2400 metres (8000 feet), it's even more important to go slowly in order to acclimatise to the high altitude. Climb no more than 450 metres (1500 feet) each day. Also, drinking plenty of water and staying hydrated can offset altitude sickness.

4. Be mindful of avalanches and falling rocks. When crossing an avalanche field, walk quickly but not so quick that you'll lose your footing. Do not stop – even for a minute – in an area where there's been a recent avalanche.

5. When you stop for the night, pitch your tent. Then take off the sweaty clothes you climbed in and put on the second, drier (and warmer) set you have in your pack. Change back into the first set for the next day's trek.

DOS AND DON'TS

✗ If you are having trouble breathing or sleeping at high altitudes or if you are light-headed, nauseous or vomiting you may have altitude sickness. Don't go any higher. In fact, it's a good idea to descend at least 300 metres (1000 feet) and stay there to acclimatise for 24 hours.

FLY A PLANE

I don't want to get too technical here but there are only two things you can deduce if you're in a plane at 35,000 feet and the flight attendant asks if anyone knows how to fly. One, she's looking for references to a good flight school, or two, the pilot is incapacitated, maybe even dead. Without getting into details, I might venture a guess at the latter. You should never attempt to fly a plane without the necessary training and qualifications, but in this case, facing imminent death, what are you going to do? Sit there and wait for the bucket of bolts you're in to fall out of the sky like a wounded duck or get yourself into the cockpit and grab the controls? Again, I'd go with the second option.

WHAT TO DO

1. Before you can think about flying you must first remove the pilot from the seat, especially if he is slumped onto the steering stick (known as the 'yoke'). If he is slumped onto the yoke then remove him quickly. Likely, the weight of his body is pushing on the yoke and the plane is descending rapidly – also known as 'going into a nose dive'.

2. If he isn't touching the yoke and the plane seems to be flying just fine, that's a good thing. It means the plane is on autopilot. Do not touch the yoke if the plane is on autopilot. It will turn off the autopilot and then you really will have to fly the plane and sooner than you want. If the plane is on autopilot go to step 4.

3. If you have to fly immediately, the first thing you have to do is level the aircraft. Find the 'altitude indicator'. Newer aircraft will have it on a computer screen. You can find it on older planes in the top row of instruments, usually in the centre. It will have a set of miniature wings and a picture of the horizon. Use the yoke to correct the pitch (climb or descend) and to bank (left or right turns). Pulling back on the yoke brings the nose up and pushing it forward brings the nose down.

4. Once you've levelled the plane, use the radio and call for help. The standard message is to repeat 'Mayday' three times followed by a description of the situation you're in (e.g. 'I'm just a regular guy who wants to help these people get home safely and I'll refuse any compensation should you offer it to me'). Use the frequency 121.50 MHz if you can. If not, send your message anyway. You should also engage the plane's transponder, which is found on or near the radio. Set its numbers to 7700 and that will send an emergency signal to nearby air traffic controllers.

5. Once you get in touch with someone, they'll ask you tons of detailed questions and give you instructions on where and how to land at the nearest airport.

continued on next page

continued

6. If you can't get in touch with anyone and you have to land the plane immediately, try to find a flat open space like a field or a road. Whatever you do, avoid places with overhead electrical wires or trees. Buildings and houses won't help you either. Bring the plane down slowly and steadily and right before you land, raise the nose up – this is called 'flaring' the nose – so that you land on the main wheels rather than the front ones.

7. Once you touch down, find the throttle, which is a black lever between the two front seats of larger aircraft, and pull it all the way back towards you. This reduces the jet power to idle.

8. Next use both feet to gently push on the pedals near your feet to brake the plane. You don't want to stamp on the breaks because the plane will skid. Just step on them with enough pressure to slow down and stop.

TIP

✓ One important control panel is the airspeed indicator. It's usually located toward the upper left of the instrument panel. Don't worry so much about how fast you're going. Just make sure the needle stays in the green area until you can get a professional on the radio. If the needle is above the green that means the airspeed is increasing and you're going down, in which case you need to pull back on the yoke. If the needle is below the green that means you're going up and decreasing speed so you need to push the nose down to level off.

LEARN PARKOUR

Parkour is a type of movement or martial arts that was invented in France by David Belle in 1988. It could be called the art of overcoming obstacles – literally. Heroes who employ parkour techniques can run up walls, leap from roof to roof and climb along narrow ledges with the speed of a cat. While athleticism is a must, parkour also takes a mental philosophy of overcoming obstacles as well. You have to trust in yourself that you can do the heroic and the impossible. Parkour techniques are the most efficient way to ensure you evade capture or to follow in the steps of James Bond as he heroically leaped over and around buildings to chase down the bad guy in *Casino Royale*.

WHAT TO DO

1. There aren't many predetermined moves in parkour because each obstacle presents its own set of unique challenges and each person's body type and energy level is different, but momentum and efficiency are the most important elements of the practice. The key is to get over or around obstacles as quickly as possible and then use your physical momentum to help with the next obstacle.

2. One must also learn how to redistribute bodily impacts to protect the legs and back. One common technique used in parkour is the body roll. Land on the balls of your feet with your knees bent but roll forwards onto the back of one shoulder and up onto the feet. This lessens the impact on your feet and legs and it uses momentum to get you up and running immediately.

3. The cat walk is a common parkour move in which you move quickly on hands and feet along a narrow ledge or walkway. Other specific techniques include vaults, drops, balances, climb ups and dismounts.

CHAPTER

3

CHIVALRY

Chivalry is not dead but it may have taken on a different look and feel than it used to have. After all, lots of women these days will take offence if you assume that opening a door for them or picking up the dinner tab means they can't take care of themselves. In fact, don't be surprised if they pick up the tab or open the door for you! All that said, when it comes to chivalrous behaviour, there are no gender barriers. A hero comes to the rescue of whoever needs rescuing. So it is that he is chivalrous to everyone he meets.

HOW TO TREAT A LADY

Though most women want to feel they are your equal, most also appreciate you going out of your way to give them special attention. Some people call this old-fashioned. Others call it smart. Being chivalrous to women is smart and heroic but if you have someone special you need to take chivalry to the next level. In other words, you need to show her you love her. But how?

Rules for chivalrous acts

1. Open doors for her. Stand to the side and let her walk through first.
2. Help her with her coat. Hold the coat by the shoulders while standing behind her. Give her time to slip her arms in.
3. Help with her seat. Pull the chair out, wait for her to sit completely, then gently push the chair back.
4. Give up your seat. Do this always for girls and elderly or obviously frail individuals of either sex.
5. Stand when a female enters or exits the room. This applies to elderly and VIP people as well.
6. Ask if she needs anything. Be attentive.
7. Pay for the date if you invited her.
8. Be honest.
9. Give flowers – lots of them and often.
10. Pay her a compliment, even if it's just to say 'lovely dress' or 'your hair looks beautiful'.

ART OF THE SERENADE

The art of the serenade is truly a lost one – which is a shame for us men because if you're truly after a woman's heart, nothing will get there faster than a performance under her window. Of course, this is the kind of heroic act that will never be forgotten so don't just go around serenading every woman you have a crush on. Think long-term here.

WHAT TO DO

1. Choose some musical accompaniment. Guitar is the traditional choice. Even if you can't play, it's okay to ask a friend to come and play while you sing. Do not, however, get someone else to sing for you. You'll actually lose the girl that way.
2. Do try and play under her window – or a window in her house. This could become a security concern so try to set it up ahead of time by talking to neighbours and housemates and the like. Just tell everyone not to let the object of your affection in on it. Surprise is an important part of a serenade.
3. Practise ahead of time. Obviously you'll want to perform a song with some love-poem-ish lyrics. Writing your own song would be the ultimate hero's serenade.
4. Serenade at dusk or thereabouts. Make sure you know her schedule and she will actually be at home.
5. When the time comes, give her a call from your mobile phone and tell her to come to her window – you have a surprise. Then start the serenade without waiting for her to get there.
6. When the song is over, don't just walk away. At least ask her out. This being a serenade you might want to ask her to marry you.

COOK A ROMANTIC DINNER

Cooking has always been a great way to a woman's heart but not if you serve hot dogs with a side of chips. Perhaps that may have been heroic when you were at university and had nothing but a hot plate to cook on but it doesn't pass muster in the dangerous world of real heroes. But then, what you serve is only half the effort. The other half is how you act. Real heroes won't spend the whole night talking about themselves, getting drunk or chewing with their mouths open. They stay attentive, ask lots of questions, and always try to create an easy atmosphere with engaging conversation and a little culinary know-how. You are, after all, trying to impress here.

WHAT TO DO

1. First off is planning, and the most important decision is what you'll eat. The food should be light and refreshing rather than heavy and rich – the latter can bring on bloating, gas and heartburn, none of which is romantic. Also, keep it simple, serve small portions, avoid red meat and don't be afraid of the vegetable. Vegetables are your friends.

2. Don't forget the wine. A romantic dinner must include wine and a heroic romantic dinner must include good wine. A Pinot Grigio or Sauvignon Blanc would complement a fish dinner, as would a light Pinot Noir. Spend a decent sum on each bottle. There's no need to have a whole case on hand but do have two or three bottles just in case. Also, try a dessert wine or aperitif after pudding.

3. Create a relaxing atmosphere with comfortable, dim lighting and low music of the jazz persuasion. Candles on the table are a must. Have flowers in a vase to add some spirit to the scene.

4. Have any entrées or salads pre-made before she arrives. Make sure the wine is already chilled and the music going as well.
5. Prep the food before she arrives but plan to cook it when she gets there. You don't want to rush into dinner and cooking is a fun thing to do. Don't expect her to help but if she wants to let her.
6. When it's time to eat, take your time over dinner. One of the most romantic things about a romantic dinner is good conversation.
7. When you're done eating, don't bother cleaning up. You – or the two of you – can do that in the morning.

REVIVE A FAINTED GIRL

Reviving a fainted woman is a lost art in more ways than one, mostly because women rarely faint any more, if they ever really did outside the movies, but it's always good to be prepared should a lady swoon in your presence. Technically speaking fainting is what happens to a person when a lack of blood and oxygen to the brain causes them to black out. This can happen to someone if they're exerting themselves on too little food, water or sleep, which means you're likely to run across fainting women late on Saturday night at the dance club. Here's what to do if that happens.

You will need

pillow, or other folded material

cold, wet handkerchief

HOW TO

1. Call a doctor
2. Elevate the fallen woman's legs with a pillow or a folded up jacket, table cloth or other material.
3. Turn the woman's head to one side and place a cold, wet handkerchief on her forehead and cheeks. Keep the kerchief wet with cool water until the doctor arrives or until she regains consciousness, usually within a few minutes.
4. If the woman comes round before the doctor arrives, help her to sit up and give her sips of cold water. Explain that everything is fine and under control.
5. Then let her lay back down and rest until the doctor arrives.

SWEEP A GIRL OFF HER FEET

If asking a girl to dance the tango (see page 56) doesn't sweep her off her feet, then you're in trouble. Then again, if you must do your sweeping at a location that does not include a dance floor, mood lights and a violin then you'll have to resort to different methods. Consider the following romantic ideas if she doesn't take the dance card.

WHAT TO DO

1. Take a stroll through the local botanical gardens. Get a book describing some of the plants and flowers you might run across so the two of you can discover them together.
2. Invite her over for a cosy evening drinking hot toddies and talking about your dreams around a fireplace.
3. Go to a museum or spend a morning visiting art galleries. Then take her out to lunch and talk about the art.
4. Get some poster board and some wooden stakes and write a series of love notes. Then stake these notes in the ground along the side of the road she takes to work. Be sure and write things you know she'll recognise as being specifically for her.
5. Send her a singing messenger to deliver a favourite poem or special message.
6. Cook a romantic dinner together. Few things work better than this, especially if you're preparing the food together.
7. See a romantic play together. Romeo and Juliet played out on stage is always a good bet.

DANCE THE TANGO

If you want to learn how to tango you can't do it from the pages of a book. This is a complicated dance with lots of particulars, but that's why it's a hero's dance. So, the only way to really learn is to get an instructor (or at least a 'how to tango' video) and get some practice. That said you could probably do with some tips for the basics and you do need to get in the right mindset before tangoing.

WHAT TO DO

1. You're going to step on some toes and make lots of mistakes so don't have a tender ego. Few men actually try the tango and if you're one who does, that's a victory in and of itself.
2. Find a partner who moves well with you, preferably one who likes to dance. What you don't want is a woman who wants to try to lead. It won't work – the man leads this dance, and there are no exceptions.
3. Posture is important. The smooth fluidity of movement, the stealthy step performed on the balls of the feet – not the tiptoes – produces the perfect posture for this dance. You will know when you've got the right posture because if it feels good, it is sure to look good.
4. Arm position is also key. Your arms should be straight and steady. Keep a firm and steady hold on your partner, but not a vice-like grip that slowly crushes their bones and dancing spirit.
5. Watch the traffic. The dance floor is likely to be filled with unpredictable dancing couples. Keep a vigilant watch for rogue couples to avoid continual interruptions of bumps and crashes.

HOST A PARTY

As the host of a party, a hero must make sure the evening goes off without a hiccup. Putting out drinks and food and getting a bunch of friends together is one thing. Keeping the conversation lively, the music great and the drinks and dinner plates full all at the same time is another. If you can pull all that off with aplomb – and give heroic first aid if and when it's needed – then you've created a masterpiece people will talk about for weeks after.

Big parties tend to take on lives of their own and all you have to do is guide the chaos, at least until midnight. What makes unpredictable evenings so smooth and fun is the work you do ahead of time. Before anyone shows up, make sure you get the fridge fully stocked with drinks (order your beer at least two days ahead of time). For food, place inviting bowls of snacks strategically around the house. Also, go ahead and check your first aid kit to make sure it's updated and within easy reach.

As soon as guests arrive offer to take their coats and give them a drink – it's a simple enough task. Things get tricky when you start having to remember names. Plus, it's always impressive to know a little something about each guest so you can offer nuggets of information when you introduce people who don't know each other. 'Judy, this is Alan,' you might say. 'Alan recently talked a suicide jumper off a ledge.' That should be enough to get them going while you peel off to work the rest of the room.

On the flip side it's also your job to keep certain guests apart. If you see a friend cornered by someone who won't stop talking, you have to get in there and break up the hostage situation. And don't just let quiet folk wander around aimlessly. Bring them into the fold and make sure they're having fun.

MAKE THE PERFECT MARTINI

Knowing how to make the perfect Martini is an impressive addition to a repertoire of heroic accomplishments. Just don't drink more than two before rescuing the neighbour's cat or less than two before tangoing.

You will need

gin (vodka can be substituted)

dry vermouth

cocktail shaker

olives

HOW TO

1. Pour the gin over ice in a cocktail shaker (stir the gin, rather than shake it so that the gin doesn't bruise) before removing the vermouth from the shelf.
2. Briefly swirl the smallest touch of vermouth in the glass before tossing out the excess – you want just enough in there to rid the gin of its bland watery complexion.
3. Strain the gin into the glass.
4. Drop in two olives and serve the drink.

LOOK AFTER A DRUNKEN COMPANION

If you and a date hit the town and she ends up drinking more than her share of wine – and I'm talking throwing-up-in-her-mouth-and-coming-on-to-the-parking-attendant-type drunk – then it's up to you to take care of her. You need to get her home and in bed – alone – before something more than her pride gets damaged. You may not be going out on another date together but that's no reason you should leave her on the street and to total ruin. Frequently, there's nothing in it for a hero but he does it anyway.

WHAT TO DO

1. Once you realise things are out of control, your goal is to take her home either by car or by taxi. If you're in the middle of dinner or at a dinner party, doing this is going to take some skill and tact. Most people at a small party will be able to tell she's hammered but don't make fun of the situation. Just stay calm and in control and explain that she needs to sleep it off at home.

2. If she's dancing with the parking attendant, be nice but firm and tell her (and him) that it's time to go. If he tries to confront you, turn to the page on avoiding confrontation (see page 63). Then suck it up and walk away. Remember your goal is to get her home.

3. Hold her hair back if she throws up. You might not go out with her again but she'll still appreciate your heroic gentlemanliness.

4. If she makes a pass at you, just say you think it would be best if you waited on that. Once you get her home, make sure she can get into her house or apartment and say goodbye at the front door and leave.

HELP SOMEONE ACROSS A ROAD

Sometimes the kindest gesture is the most heroic regardless of its level of difficulty or danger. When an elderly lady or man is crossing a large, busy road it can seem quite harrowing to them and very gracious when a young man helps carry a heavy grocery bag while holding the cars at bay. It's the small things that make everyday heroes.

WHAT TO DO

1. When you approach someone on the street, always be polite and humble. Ask if you can help rather than just grabbing a bag, which can startle someone.
2. While you're waiting to cross you can tell the person what will happen when the light changes again. Say, 'Okay, this isn't a very long light so let's try to go as fast as we can, but don't worry if we don't get to the other side in time. I'll make sure those cars stay put until we get there.'
3. When you walk, stay with the person you're helping across the road rather than taking off ahead of them. Offer your arm if they need something to hold on to.
4. If you don't make it to the other side before the light changes, simply hold your hand up in a 'hold on a minute' way to the cars waiting at the traffic signal. No one's going to mow you down. You just want to put your hand up to get their attention.
5. When you get to the other side, make sure they will be okay from there on out, and go on your way.

BE A GOOD SPORT

Sport often imitates life, so being a hero on the football field, the tennis court or the cricket pitch is good practice for playing the right way at the office or in a relationship. Practice, hard work and respect for the people you're competing against are the heroic gestures when you're in friendly competition with others – not winning at all costs. That said, if you play heroically, winning is always that much sweeter.

WHAT TO DO

1. Make sure everyone knows what the rules are before you start the game.
2. Pick on someone your own size.
3. Don't stand and celebrate when someone on the opposing team gets hurt. Lend a helping hand.
4. When the opposing team or player makes a good play, let them know it. There's no reason to go overboard. A simple 'nice play' will do.
5. Competition can really boost adrenaline and that can lead to angry confrontations. Try to keep your emotions in check. It's only a game.
6. Always congratulate the opposing team or player whether you win or lose.

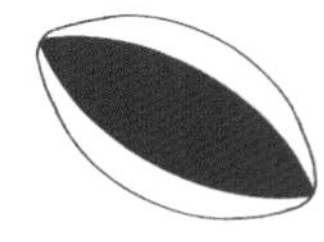

STAY OUT OF FIGHTS

Most people think that heroes are big, beefy brutes ready to fight the bad guys at a moment's notice but that's not always true. You don't have to be big, beefy or brutish to be a hero. Nor do you have to fight. Especially if the bad guy is bigger and more beefy and brutish than you are. Tussling with such a guy would not be heroic. It would be stupid. Of course, if life and limb depend on it, no mountain is too high to climb for a true hero, but if you can avoid confrontation, that is often the best way to go. Here's how to grit your teeth and bear it.

WHAT TO DO

1. Don't sweat the small stuff. There will always be people in your life who are annoying. That doesn't mean you have to let it bother you.
2. Bite your tongue. Again, rude, irritating people abound but you don't have to tell them that. Patience is one of the hardest virtues to embrace.
3. If you do have to say something, think before you talk. Take mental notes on what the person is doing that is so annoying so if an eventual confrontation has to happen at some point, you'll be prepared to point out his offences.
4. If confrontation does result in words being exchanged, be careful and conscious with your words. In the heat of the moment, you're liable to say things you don't really mean, which is no good when you're saying those things to a friend and really no good if you're saying them to a mean person with biceps the size of your thighs.

CHAPTER

4

EMERGENCY EXPERTISE

No one likes an emergency though some men relish any opportunity to spring into action and help those who cannot help themselves. Some may mistake this as taking pleasure in chaos and destruction but it's actually just the opposite. Heroes know that accidents and emergencies can happen and they take pride in their emergency life-saving skills, watching out for the weary and reclaiming order where there is none.

FIRST AID

An essential skill for any hero during an emergency is knowing how to give first aid. One of the best ways to provide calm in an emergency is to be able to treat a badly injured person. Not only can you help to save someone's life but when others see you attending to the person, they'll calm down if they think someone knows what to do. It helps to keep some emergency first aid kits around, such as in your house and in your car, so that you're always prepared. Of course you're not going to have a whole range of medical equipment, but there are some basic items that will always be useful.

Basic first aid kit	
First aid manual	Blister pad
Adhesive bandages	Aspirin, Paracetamol or Ibuprofen
Gauze pads	Snake bite kit
Triangle bandage	Antiseptic cream
Elasticated bandage	Razor blade
Athletic tape	

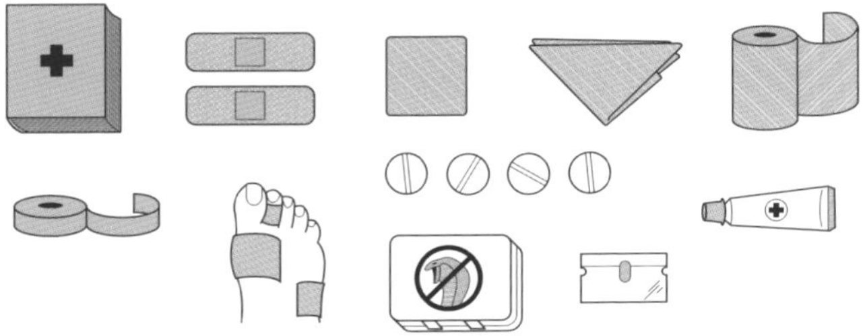

BROKEN LIMBS

Broken bones happen more often than people might think. Even a cracked little finger can be painful and debilitating. With some basic first aid techniques you can get a person out of more danger and into the arms of a professional without exacerbating the injury.

You will need

gauze pads

two stiff objects (boards, sticks) to use as splints

string, rope, belts or strips of cloth

HOW TO

1. The only accurate way to determine if a bone is broken is to X-ray it. If you or the victim suspect there's a broken bone, treat it as such.
2. Broken bones can pierce the skin. If you see this, hold on to your lunch and don't touch. You don't want to risk infection. You do, however, want to stop the bleeding by applying steady pressure to the area with a sterile gauze pad.
3. You need to stabilise the limb with a splint. Put the splints on the sides of the limb that is broken. Make sure that they are longer than the injured limb.
4. Tie anything that is available (string, rope, belts strips of torn cloth) around the splints to keep them in place on the limb. Don't tie the splints too tightly to avoid cutting off circulation.
5. Test the tightness by placing two fingers under the ties. If you can't fit them, loosen the ties.

BULLET AND STAB WOUNDS

More rare than a broken bone but not out of the question, a violent injury, such as a bullet wound or a stabbing, requires fast action.

You will need

clean cloth or a sterile bandage

splint

sterile dressing

HOW TO

1. If someone staggers into your front yard with a knife in his side or a shard of glass stuck in his arm, your first instinct might be to run inside. But this is a book about heroes so hold your ground. Your second instinct might then be to pull out the embedded object. Don't do this either. Sometimes objects embedded into penetrating wounds help to reduce the bleeding and the act of pulling them out can cause more severe bleeding.
2. Call your local emergency services and try to elevate the injured area to cut down on the bleeding.
3. For bullet wounds or stab wounds that aren't blocked by a knife or other sharp object, try to stop or control the blood flow using direct pressure with a clean cloth, sterile bandage, shirt or anything else on hand – even if it's your actual hand.
4. Elevate the wound and try to immobilise the injured area either with a gauze dressing or, if it's a limb, by making a splint. This will encourage the wound to start clotting and prevent further injury.

5. If the bleeding will not stop then consider a tourniquet – a band of cloth or a belt that is tied on the heart side of a wound and twisted until the flow of blood is shut off. This should only be done as a last resort – as a measure to save a person's life. That's because after about ten minutes tourniquets cause permanent vascular and/or nerve damage, which means the limb the tourniquet is on will have to be amputated.

BURNS

It can be all too easy to get a nasty burn – cooking dinner for a pretty woman can make a man nervous, and accidents can follow. And you won't always come out unscathed when pulling someone from a burning building (see page 86). All heroes should how to treat a burn.

You will need

bowl of cold water

splint

sterile dressing

HOW TO

1. Stick your hand in a bowl of cold water right away.
2. Hold it inside the bowl while the tap continues to circulate cold water around it.
3. Place a wet cloth on the burn until the pain goes away.
4. Use a dry gauze pad and athletic tape to protect the burn from scrapes and other things that might irritate it.

SNAKEBITES

If you know you're headed into snake country, it's always good to bring along a snakebite kit so that you can use the suction extractor that comes inside it. Do not cut open the wound with a knife like in all those Westerns. You'll just end up with a knife cut as well as a snakebite to deal with.

You will need

snakebite kit

warm soapy water

bandages

HOW TO

1. If you can, get the person to a medical facility right away.
2. If you can't get to a doctor, quickly loosen any restrictive clothing and wash the wound with warm soapy water.
3. Let the wound bleed for about 30 seconds to get some of the venom out.
4. Wrap bandages 10 cm (4 inches) above and below the bite to slow the venom. This is not a tourniquet and should not cut off the blood flow; you should be able to fit a finger under the bandage.
5. Place a suction extractor over the bite and draw out the venom until there is no more discharge from the bite. If one extractor won't fit over both fang marks, switch back and forth, sucking for two minutes at a time.
6. Dress the wound with a gauze pad and tape. Immobilise the bitten area and keep the wound below or level with the heart to reduce swelling.
7. Head to a medical facility right away.

PUT OUT A FIRE

Fires are bad news. They can destroy a man's hard-earned home improvements and they will wipe out his belongings. To squelch a blaze before it gets to that point, you have to deprive it of one of its three needed ingredients: air, fuel and heat.

WHAT TO DO

1. If rubbish, carpet or wood is on fire, water will work fine.
2. For electrical and kitchen grease fires, use a blanket or sand to smother the flames.
3. Fire extinguishers are rated by size and type of fire they can put out: Class A fires are those involving materials such as wood, paper, or cloth; Class B fires are burning liquids, oils and greases; Class C fires are electrical fires; and Class D fires are those involving combustible metals.
4. To use an extinguisher, point the nozzle toward the base of the flame and start spraying.
5. Sweep the nozzle back and forth across the flame (always keeping it aimed at its base) until the fire is out.

TIP

✓ Fire extinguishers have pressure gauges that need to be checked periodically to make sure they retain enough pressure to push out the chemical fire deterrent they carry. After a fire extinguisher is used it loses all its pressure and needs to be replaced.

THE HEIMLICH MANOEUVRE

If you just spent three hours grilling up a nice fat chicken, the last thing you want is for one of your guests to choke on it. Invented in 1974 by Dr Henry Heimlich, this surefire way to unblock a choking friend's airway is now a worldwide lifesaving standard. If somebody starts to choke, they will be unable to talk, but they will motion to their throat with both hands. Give them the Heimlich manoeuvre, and your hero status is assured.

You will need

two free hands

sense of urgency

HOW TO

1. Stand behind your unlucky dinner guest and wrap your arms around his or her waist.
2. Make a fist and place the thumb side of your fist just below the choker's ribcage.
3. Hold your fist with your other hand and make quick inward and upward thrusts into the abdomen. Take care not to squeeze the ribcage with your arms while you're doing this, but focus the thrust on your hands.
4. This should expel the offending item from the victim's airway. If it doesn't, repeat the procedure until the person is breathing properly again.

DOS AND DON'TS

- ✗ Don't squeeze the ribcage, as this could lead to a broken rib.
- ✗ Don't slap the victim on the back.

SAVE YOURSELF

If you're caught out when alone you can follow the same procedure as above, or try leaning over the back of a chair or the edge of a table, thrusting your abdomen against it until you can breathe easier.

HINT

It is possible to use the Heimlich to revive a drowning person. Lay them on their back and turn their head to the side so water can drain out. Put one hand on top of the other and place the heel of the bottom hand on the victim's abdomen just under the ribcage. Lock your elbows and make quick inward and upward thrusts into the victim's abdomen until all water has drained from the mouth. At that point, if the victim is still unconscious and is not breathing, perform CPR until help arrives.

DEAL WITH A GAS LEAK

Gas leaks are a common problem after a big disaster like an earthquake or hurricane and they can be dangerous. Natural gas is non-toxic, but it can ignite if exposed to a flame or spark. If you smell gas, do the following:

WHAT TO DO

1. Extinguish all flames and put out cigarettes. Do not light matches or operate electrical appliances, as they could create a spark.
2. Call the fire department or gas company to report the smell.
3. Turn off all gas appliances and make sure their pilot lights are out as well.
4. Create ventilation by opening all windows and doors. This will reduce the chance of a gas build up. If the smell of gas is strong, go ahead and move everyone outdoors, leaving the doors open.
5. If you still think that gas is escaping, turn off the gas at its supply valve – located by the gas meter on the gas inlet pipe – by rotating the valve one quarter turn with an adjustable wrench. The valve's stem should be perpendicular to the inlet pipe to stop the flow of gas.
6. Leave the property and wait for help. If someone is feeling sick it could be carbon monoxide poisoning. Call the emergency services.

TIPS

- ✓ Pilot lights and main burners on gas appliances should always produce a blue flame. If the flame is yellow or red, something is wrong; call for service.
- ✓ Have your gas-fired equipment serviced and cleaned regularly.

STAY SAFE DURING AN EARTHQUAKE

The major earthquakes – ones that register from 7.0 to 7.9 in magnitude on the Richter scale – happen on average 18 times per year. If you live on the Pacific Rim where 80 per cent of all the earthquakes in the world happen, it doesn't hurt to know what to do when the big one hits. Here's what to do:

WHAT TO DO

1. If you're indoors, take cover under a sturdy piece of furniture and hold on to it. If there isn't a piece of furniture near you, drop to the ground, cover your head with your arms and crouch in an inside corner of the building.
2. Stay away from windows, doors, walls, lighting fixtures, furniture or anything else that could fall on you and cause injury. Only use a doorway for shelter if you know it is a load-bearing wall.
3. Stay inside until the shaking stops and it is safe to go out. DO NOT use the lifts.
4. If you're outside when an earthquake hits, find a clear spot away from buildings, trees and power lines, drop to the ground, and stay there until the shaking stops. The greatest danger exists directly outside buildings alongside exterior walls and windows or near doors where lots of people could stampede out. Collapsing walls, flying glass and falling objects cause most earthquake-related injuries.
5. If you're in a car, get out of traffic and stop. Stay in the vehicle. When the tremor stops avoid roads, bridges or ramps that may have been damaged.

MANAGE A FLOOD

Floods have been both a blessing and a curse for humans for thousands of years. The floods of the River Nile in Egypt provided some of the first fertile farm-rich soil in history along its banks. However, as more cities and towns were built in flood plains, the rising water became a problem, launching epic battles between nature and man, with nature most often winning; although that hasn't stopped us from redirecting rivers and building elaborate sea walls, dams, dykes and levies. Nevertheless, the water still comes and nature still wins more often than not. If you start hearing newsreaders talk about a Flood Watch, then you know a flood is possible. If they're talking about a Flood Warning, that means some flooding has already happened and it's going to happen in your area soon.

WHAT TO DO

1. If you hear a Flood Watch stay informed via radio or TV.
2. Prepare your house. Move your furniture and valuables to higher floors or onto higher shelves.
3. After that, prepare to evacuate. Fill your car's petrol tank in case an evacuation notice is issued and get your Emergency Kit together
4. If you have time, consider using sandbags to keep water away from your home. It takes two people about one hour to fill and place 100 sandbags, giving you a wall that is 30 cm high and 6 metres long.
5. If it does start to flood in your area, stay calm. If the water is rising rapidly, decide quickly to move to higher ground before it gets too high. You don't have to wait for official instructions to know when it's time to go. Just remember to grab your Emergency Kit.
6. Before you go, try to turn off your utilities at the main switches and disconnect as many electrical appliances as possible to guard against fire. WARNING: Do not touch electrical equipment if you are wet or are standing in water!
7. If you leave your home on foot, do not walk through moving water. 15 centimetres of moving water can make you fall. Avoid drainage channels where water can flow fast. Children in particular are in danger of getting swept into large drains.
8. If you're driving, stick to main roads and try to drive in the centre of the road where it is highest. Never drive into a side street or underpass that has standing water in it – you don't know how deep it is. If you must drive through shallow waters, keep moving slowly but surely. Letting your foot off the accelerator will allow water to enter the engine through the exhaust pipe, which will stall it. If the floodwaters begin to rise around your car, abandon it and move to higher ground if you can do so safely. You and the vehicle could be swept away.

COPE IN A BLACKOUT

Power cuts are one of the most common collateral emergencies when earthquakes and floods hit hard – and that can exacerbate already dire situations. Like most emergencies, coping with a blackout or a power cut is easier if you're prepared (those candles and flashlights in your Emergency Kit will be your best friends). That way when you get caught in the dark, you can make the hero work look easy.

WHAT TO DO

1. If the lights go out, check if your neighbours have electricity. If they do, the problem could just be a blown fuse or a tripped circuit. It would not be good for your heroic reputation if you launched an evacuation of the neighbourhood for no reason. Keep extra fuses on hand and a torch nearby to save yourself from such misery.
2. If you discover the buildings around you are affected, turn off all appliances and lights with the exception of one light fixture so that you will know when your power has been restored.
3. Check on elderly friends, relatives, or neighbours who may need assistance if the weather is severe.
4. Keep extra charcoal briquettes or propane around for your barbecue, so that you can still cook. Always make sure you have adequate ventilation – keep it outdoors.
5. Eliminate any unnecessary travel, especially by car. Often traffic signals will not work during power cuts.
6. Don't open the fridge or freezer unless absolutely necessary. They can stay cool for hours, keeping food from spoiling, unless you stand there with the door open browsing for a candlelight snack.

ORGANISE AN EVACUATION

Evacuations are serious business and a logistical nightmare. Local authorities don't ask people to leave their homes and towns unless they really mean it and imminent danger is on the way. Luckily, there's usually some warning before disaster strikes so you don't have to panic and you can organise things quickly but calmly. Of course, if you're prepared ahead of time with an Emergency Kit, it'll be smooth sailing. When there is impending disaster, be sure to keep listening to local radio and television reports. If local officials ask you to leave, do so immediately!

WHAT TO DO

1. If you have several hours before evacuation check your Emergency Kit to make sure your supplies are replenished. Then gather neighbours, family, friends and anyone you'll be evacuating into one house.
2. Call ahead to your destination to make reservations and otherwise prepare for your arrival.
3. If you have time after doing those things, protect your home by bringing in large items around your garden that might fly around and damage property. Also, turn off electricity and water and hammer plywood over outside windows to prevent them from getting broken.
4. Move television sets, computers, stereos and electronic equipment to higher levels of your home and away from windows to protect them from flooding or winds.
5. When it's time to leave, grab your Emergency Kit and go!

CHAPTER

5

DARING RESCUES

Rescue is a curious feat. On the one hand, it is truly a hero's job. On the other hand, the chances of getting yourself killed, maimed or lost increase dramatically when you run into a burning building, jump into the ocean to right a capsized boat or try to pull someone out of a hole in the thin ice. That's why the most heroic heroes think before they act – or at the very least they read this book so they know what to do when called upon for a daring rescue.

GET A CAT DOWN FROM A TREE

A true hero helps everyone out of their troubles, no matter how small or mundane the task may seem. Certainly a hero's work is not done until he can extract the elderly neighbour's furry feline friend from the high branches of the backyard oak. The neighbour's gratitude might not quite be worth the many cat scratches, but a true hero won't let that put him off.

You will need

patience

ladder

leather work gloves

pillowcase

rope

HOW TO

1. The first thing to do is to stay calm (or try to get your neighbour to stay calm). If a cat is given privacy and time it will likely come down on its own. Give it a full night. In the meantime, keep the dog inside. You can try calling to the cat at the base of the tree or opening a can of cat food to coax the beast down if you like but don't get frustrated. Cats are notorious for not listening.

2. If the cat is a kitten or it has a leash wrapped around its neck (for reasons that don't need to be disclosed) you'll have to go get it. Kittens aren't strong enough to stay up in trees in high wind for very long.

3. First try to get the cat to come down on its own by leaning a wooden ladder up against the tree next to the cat. Leave it alone with the ladder for at least 15 minutes.

4. If the cat is too freaked out to use the ladder, put on your work gloves to protect yourself from scratches and take a pillowcase and a rope up with you.

5. When you reach the cat grab it by the nape of the neck to reduce your chances of getting scratched. This also has a calming effect on the creature.

6. Gently put the cat in the pillowcase – an action which will undo the aforementioned calm – and secure it with the rope.

7. Next, lower the cat slowly to a person on the ground who is able to catch it.

8. Take the cat into the house before you let it out of the pillowcase, lest it run up the tree again in a state of panic from getting put in a pillowcase.

GET A VEHICLE OUT OF THE MUD

When travelling in the great outdoors it is surprisingly easy to find yourself on a lonely stretch of road, up to your axles in mud. It is a daunting situation but with a little ingenuity and brute strength can be overcome in no time at all.

WHAT TO DO

1. The reason you are stuck is that the tyres have too little traction to move any further. The first thing to do is try to rock the car back and forth. A slowly moving wheel can apply more surface area to the mud. Once some progress has been made, try to accelerate a little and hopefully the car will have found its own way out.

2. If this is unsuccessful, use pieces of wood or stones to form a makeshift ramp around the tyres. Once you have a solid structure, accelerate slowly over it and you should find yourself free. If there are no suitable objects – a jacket, or preferably four – can do a good job of increasing traction.

3. The last resort is to use a shovel and a lot of elbow grease. Dig a sloping area around your tyres in order to free up room and increase surface area for your tyres. If there is little traction still, repeat the above procedure.

4. If none of these methods are successful, you are well and truly stuck. Your best bet is to head off and try to find a helpful chap with an 4-wheel drive and tow bar.

ICE RESCUE

If someone breaks through thin ice, you have less than 30 minutes to get them out before severe hypothermia sets in. Act fast and whatever you do, don't fall in yourself.

You will need

long stick, rope or ladder

boat

blanket

HOW TO

1. DON'T run over to the victim. Broken ice is a very clear sign that it won't hold you either. Call your local emergency services.
2. Then get as close to the person as possible and use a long stick or rope to reach out to them. You may need to get on your stomach to reach further. This also spreads your body weight over the ice. If you hear the ice creak or groan, back up.
3. Keep talking to the victim, telling them that they're going to be all right. This has a calming effect.
4. Once they grab onto the stick or the rope, pull them to safety.
5. If there is a boat nearby use it to skate over to the victim on the ice and pull them on board. If the ice breaks then you'll be in a boat rather than at the bottom of a frozen lake.
6. Treat the victim for hypothermia. Wrap the person in a dry blanket, and get them to a hospital as soon as possible.

RESCUE SOMEONE FROM A BURNING BUILDING

Burning buildings are not great places to hang out. In fact, if you're in a building that's on fire, get out and get out quickly. At the same time, if you hear screams from inside a burning building, the only natural response for a hero is to try to help that person get out. If there are firemen around, alert them. They consider going into a burning building as the most dangerous job they do, but at least they have the fireproof clothes, oxygen masks, tools and training to go in safely. You don't. Besides, firemen on the scene won't let you into the building anyway. If there are no firemen present or if you're already inside a burning building and you need to help someone get out, try the following steps.

WHAT TO DO

1. Smoke is as much a killer as than fire, if not more, so stay low to the ground – smoke rises.
2. Take a rope or electrical cable with you and feed it out behind you as you go so that you can find your way back to the door or window you came in if the building fills with smoke.
3. If you don't have rope or a cable, and you can't see your toes when standing upright, get on your hands and knees and use your hand to follow a wall into the building.
4. Take note of additional windows in case you need to make a quick exit.
5. Call out for the trapped person as you go and see if you can determine where they are. If they can't tell you, simply follow the sound of their voice.
6. If you get to a person and they are unconscious, there is a chance they will have a head or neck injury. Moving them in a jarring fashion may injure them further. On the other hand, if you leave them they will have less of a chance of survival. One option is to find a blanket, roll them onto it, fold the sides over the body, and drag the person out head first. Another option is to hoist them over one shoulder and carry them out by standing on their feet and pulling them up to your chest and shoulder with their hands.
7. Always leave a burning building by the path you came in if possible. If that path is blocked, exit through the nearest window. If you're on a higher floor and you can't get down, open a window and straddle the windowsill, putting one leg out and waving with one arm. This is an old firefighting signal for help and if there are firemen on the ground they'll raise a ladder to you.

RESCUE A DROWNING PERSON

Drowning is not good for your health and it should be avoided at all costs. For some, though, it's not that easy. Children who don't know how to swim fall into swimming pools and rushing rivers can catch even the strongest swimmers off guard. Even your pet dog can get in over his head if he wants that stick bad enough. Knowing how to save someone from drowning is essential if you spend any amount of time around water. But remember, someone who is drowning is often panicking – this can pose grave danger to themselves as well as to their rescuer. If you get close they'll grab and flail and could take you down with them. For this reason, only swim out to save a drowning person as a last resort. First try reaching out to them with a stick or tossing them something that floats.

You will need

length of rope

towel

long stick or boat oar

something that floats (cooler bag, spare tyre, pool float)

boat

HOW TO

1. If the person is conscious and close enough to the shore or edge of the pool, stand with your feet apart or lay on your stomach to prevent the victim from pulling you into the water, and reach out to them with anything they can grab onto like a long stick or even a rope (though most ropes will sink rather quickly).

2. Talk to them and tell them in a loud, firm voice to grab onto the thing you're extending out to them. Once they grab it, pull them to shore.

3. If they're further out, find something that floats to throw to them such as a life jacket, an ice chest, or the spare tyre in your car.
4. If they are too far out to reach with a stick or a float you can either get in a boat or, as a last resort, get in the water and swim out to them.
5. If you do have to get in the water to save someone, swim up to them from behind while talking to them. Tell them you're going to pull them to safety. Often your voice will have a calming effect.
6. When you reach the victim whack them in the head with a club to knock them out. Just kidding. Simply approach the person from behind, if possible, and hook your arm over their chest as you sidestroke back to shore. Tell the person to relax and float on their back.
7. If, once you've reached the shore or have the victim on board the boat, the person is unconscious, act fast with your first aid skills and you could save a life. They may appear dead, but often that's not the case.

CARDIOPULMONARY RESUSCITATION (CPR)

There are many things that could cause a person to stop breathing and his heart stop beating. Heart attack, near-drowning, choking, drug overdose and electric shock are just a few. When this happens you can keep a person alive with CPR long enough for professional help to arrive.

You will need

telephone

basic knowledge of CPR technique

willingness to put your mouth on a stranger's mouth (male or female)

HOW TO

1. Call your local emergency services.
2. With the victim lying on his or her back, tilt the head back, lift the chin and check for breathing by listening closely, while looking to see if the chest is rising and falling.
3. Check to see that nothing, including the tongue, is blocking the victim's air passage, thus preventing them from breathing. If you see that they're choking on something, give them the Heimlich manoeuvre or clear the object away with your finger.
4. If they're still not breathing, give mouth-to-mouth resuscitation. For this, the victim should be lying on his or her back, chin up.
5. Place two fingers gently under the chin to keep the head back. Place your other hand on the victim's forehead, using the thumb and index finger to pinch the nose closed.

6. Blow forcefully into the victim's mouth, making sure to cover the mouth with your lips so that no air escapes. You will be able to see the chest rise when you blow and fall when you stop. Repeat.

7. If the person is able to breathe on their own, stop. If not, check for a pulse by placing two fingers on the neck just to the left or right of, and slightly up from the Adam's apple. If there is a pulse, continue mouth-to-mouth until the victim can breathe or until help arrives.

8. If there is no pulse, put the heel of one hand at the centre of the victim's chest, just on top of the breastbone. Put your other hand on top of it and interlace the fingers.

9. With your shoulders directly over your hands and your elbows straight, push down firmly on the chest by about 5 cm (2 in). Wait half a second and release. Repeat this 15 times.

10. After 15 pumps, give two more breaths. Continue 15 pumps and two breaths until help arrives.

DOS AND DON'TS

✗ Do not give CPR to someone who doesn't need it. You could seriously injure them even more than they already are.

✓ Do check frequently to make sure they're breathing on their own. If they are, you can stop CPR.

MOUNTAIN RESCUE

A mountain rescue is not for the weak at heart. Nor is it for the wobbly-kneed. Then again, neither is mountain climbing. To get someone off a cliff or down off the mountain after a bad fall, you'll need a sound knowledge of outdoor survival skills and first aid. Furthermore, it wouldn't hurt you to have a sturdy grasp on how to use a climbing rope.

You will need

- **first aid kit**
- **climbing rope**
- **climbing harness**
- **stick or similar for splints**
- **clothing for slings and padding**
- **stretcher or litter**

HOW TO

1. Before bounding out onto an icy cliff or across a slippery snowfield to save someone, make sure of your own safety and determine how the rescue will unfold once you reach the victim.
2. If you're on a rope, it's very important to tell whoever you're rescuing to stay calm and to stand away from any drop offs. The closer you get, let them know what you plan to do.
3. Administer first aid before doing anything else. If the person cannot walk, do not move them unless they are in imminent danger. If they must be moved, stabilise any broken bones with a splint.
4. Support a broken upper arm with a sling. Fold a large piece of cloth into a triangle. Slide the wide part of the triangle under the injured arm and tie the loose ends around the victim's neck.

5. If either a forearm or wrist is fractured, wrap something rigid, say a small stick, with clothing and tie it around the arm – either side of the injured area – with cloth strips. Then make a sling.

6. A splint for the lower leg can be made in the same way. Place a board or stick on either side of the leg – both extending from groin to heel. Pad the injury well and tie the boards in place at the groin, thigh, knee and ankle.

7. To transport a seriously injured person off a mountain, you will need a stretcher or litter along with several more ropes. Always move slowly and take the safest and easiest route down, not necessarily the quickest.

CHAPTER

6

PERSONAL SURVIVAL

Saving others is a hero's natural modus operandi but there's not much of a chance to pull someone from a hole in the ice if you fall in first. In other words, if you don't take the time to save yourself you can forget about saving others. A hero needs to learn all the skills that will help him survive when he is wandering the wilderness on his own, so intrepid explorers or heroes whose middle name is 'Adventure' should take particular notice of this chapter.

FIND WATER

While you may be hungry enough to eat a horse, it's always best to find water first. A man can last up to ten days without food, but a day or two without water is bad news. Finding water is mostly about looking in the right places.

You will need

rubber hose

cloth

container

water purification tablets

knife or machete

HOW TO

1. Fresh water collects in rock crevices and tree hollows. Siphon the water out or use a dipper to scoop it out. If the water is difficult to retrieve, dip a cloth into the water and then wring it out.
2. Purify any water you collect with iodine tablets or boil it for three to five minutes.
3. Ice and snow are good sources of water but melt them first to avoid losing body heat and suffering diarrhoea.
4. Cut off the top of a cactus to access the pulp inside. Squeeze the water out into a container.
5. Bamboo collects water. Bend the top of a stalk over a container and cut it open.
6. Banana trees are also a good source of water. Cut the tree down about 15 cm (6 in) above the ground and dig out a bowl in the stump, where water will collect from the tree's roots.

FIND YOUR WAY WITHOUT A COMPASS

There's no shame in getting lost. Some of history's greatest heroes have done it (think of Columbus). What will blemish your image as a hero in the great outdoors is not being able to find your way home. You don't need a map or a compass to do it, all you have to know is how to find north.

WHAT TO DO

1. A watch can be made into a compass. Hold it horizontal to the ground and point the hour hand directly at the sun. Then imagine a line bisecting the hour hand and the 12 o'clock mark on your watch. The top of the line points south in the northern hemisphere, and north in the southern hemisphere.

2. If you only have a digital watch, just note the time and draw out a watch with hands, either on paper with a pencil or even in the dirt with a stick and apply the above principals.

3. If you don't have a watch, find a straight stick, about 1 metre (3 ft) tall, and plant it straight in level ground so it casts back a shadow. Mark the tip of this shadow with a stone. This will be your west mark. Wait 15 minutes, then go back and check the shadow's progress, as it will have moved. Mark the new shadow tip with another stone and you will have an east mark. Draw a line between the two marks for a west/east line. Draw another line exactly perpendicular to this one to form a north/south line. By placing your left foot at the west mark and your right foot at the east mark you will always be facing north. This rule applies both in the northern and southern hemispheres.

continued over page

continued

4. If you're lost at night, you can navigate by the stars. In the northern hemisphere, find the North Star by locating the Plough. Make an imaginary line using the two stars that form its front lip and continue this line about 5 times its original length. You should arrive at the North Star. Now just draw an imaginary line from the North Star down to earth and this is your northerly direction.

5. In the southern hemisphere, you need to locate the Southern Cross. Once you've picked it out, look to the two stars that make the longer of the two crossbeams. Extend this crossbeam out at least five times itself and mark that imaginary point in the sky. A line brought down to earth from that point will give you an approximate south reading.

DOS AND DON'TS

✗ Do not try to walk in a straight line, believing that you will not waver from the correct course. Instead, mark a point on the horizon and head toward it. Once there, repeat your chosen navigational method.

✗ Do not panic if the sky is overcast. Not only is this rather un-heroic but unnecessary. You must wait and hope for a break in the cloud, if this occurs be swift and get as good a marker as possible.

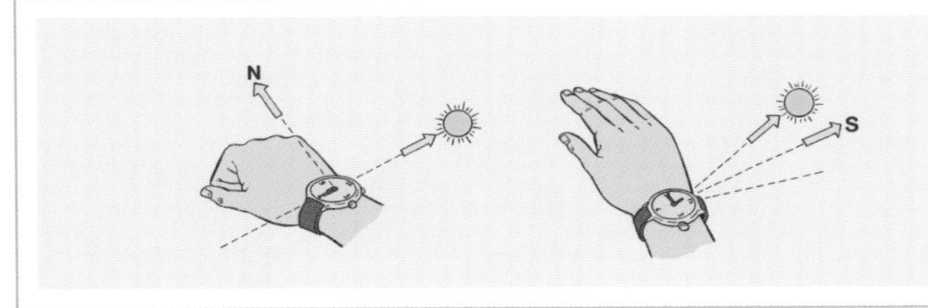

START A FIRE

If you don't happen to have a lighter or some dry matches with you, then all is not lost – there are other ways to start a fire. You can try getting a spark with flint and steel, or use a magnifying glass to focus a concentrated ray of sunlight on to a dry nest of tinder. Failing that you can do it the really difficult way – by rubbing two sticks together.

You will need

straight stick of hardwood (the drill)

flat piece of dry, dead, softwood (the fire board)

hand-sized piece of hardwood (the socket)

bootlace

50-cm (1½-ft) curved stick (the bow)

dried grass, pine needles, and twigs for kindling

HOW TO

1. Whittle one end of the drill into a point and round off the other end.
2. Cut a small hole halfway along the fire board and a few centimetres from its edge. The hole should be big enough to fit the rounded end of the drill inside.
3. Then cut a triangular notch in the fire board from the hole to the nearest edge. This will serve as a channel for ashes and embers to spill out and onto your kindling.
4. You are going to use the socket to press down firmly on the drill. To stop it from slipping, cut a small hole in the socket so that the pointed end of the drill will fit there snugly.
5. Tie your bootlace loosely onto each end of the bow so that you'll be able to loop it over the drill.
6. Rest the fire board on the ground so that the notched side is in contact with a small,

but tight, nest of kindling. Place the round end of the drill in the hole in the fire board and hold it in place firmly with the socket.

7. Make sawing motions with the bow to work the drill back and forth in a not-too-fast, not-too-slow, steady rhythm. Make sure the drill stays in contact with the fire board. Eventually, the friction will cause smoke to form and embers should start rolling down the notch and into the nest of kindling.

8. When this happens, add more dried grass to the pile of kindling and blow gently to ignite the ember into flames. Then work quickly and carefully to build up the fire.

DOS AND DON'TS

✗ Don't get discouraged as this can take a long time to accomplish. The good thing is you'll get nice and toasty from all the exercise.

✗ Don't forget to collect plenty of firewood before you start trying to get an ember.

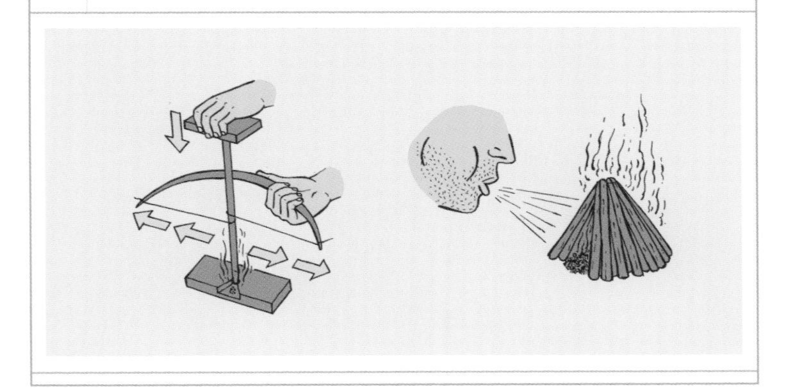

MAKE A SHELTER

Even if you know how to navigate your way home, you may still have to find food, water and some shelter before you can get there. If you need shelter, try building a lean-to, which is a 'wall' of natural materials propped up against a tree or stone.

You will need

branches and sticks

straight poles

boughs

mud

rope or tough vines

HOW TO

1. To make a lean-to all you need are some wrist-sized pieces of wood and some boughs or branches.
2. Make a large rectangle on the ground with your branches and lash them together at the corners.
3. Fill in the area with smaller pieces of wood lashed together.
4. Lay the structure against a tree or rock and cover the outside with branches or boughs. It might be helpful to weave the branches into the sticks below.

RIGHT A CAPSIZED BOAT

If you're on a big sailboat – say 6 m (20 ft) or over – and it capsizes then the most heroic thing you can do is to find something that floats and hold on tight until help arrives. There's no way one person can right a large sailboat in open water. Can't happen. Small dinghies, on the other hand, are a different matter. Should one go over, strap on a life jacket and get into the drink. It's time to put your heroic girth to work.

You will need

capsized dinghy

all your body weight

HOW TO

1. Climb on top of the overturned boat and position yourself to one side of the centreboard or keel.
2. Grab the tip of the keel and hang off it. If you can't get the boat to right itself, try standing on the keel near the hull. Don't stand too close to the tip of the keel or you risk snapping it off.
3. Once the boat begins to roll continue to push down on the keel with your body weight and your feet.
4. When the keel dips into the water, grab the side of the boat and pull it down. Try to lift yourself onto the edge of the boat so that you're in the boat when it settles back onto its hull. If you don't get in the boat at this point, be sure to move away from the boat when it comes completely over so you don't get stuck underneath.

EVADE CAPTURE

You can't always overpower the bad guys, especially if you're outnumbered. In fact, brute strength is not necessarily a hero's most important attribute. He has to be clever – and sometimes clever means getting out of danger and re-grouping. If you're in enemy territory and they're on to you, the one thing you don't want to do is get caught. Here's how to make sure that doesn't happen.

WHAT TO DO

- ✓ In situations in which you are in immediate danger, you must hide and stay quiet. However, try not to hide in a place with only one opening – you don't want to get cornered. Fields of tall grass or mature corn stalks are excellent hiding places if you're outdoors.
- ✓ You can't stay in one place to be successful at getting away from the bad guys. After the initial danger is over and you've hidden successfully, get moving. Try sliding into rivers and riding the current far downstream. Hop trains for brief rides. 'Borrow' bicycles.
- ✓ If you're in a building, try hiding out on a window ledge, then leave the building by climbing over adjacent roof tops or down fire escapes.
- ✓ Make sure you're not leaving a trail. If you're running in snow or any other ground that leaves footprints, try to cover your tracks or lead your followers astray by back-tracking.
- ✓ Evading capture while in a car is more difficult than if you are on foot. Cars can't be hidden as easily. Try leading your assailants into a neighbourhood with small streets – it helps if you're familiar with the neighbourhood. Take frequent turns. Look for alleys or garages you can pull into without being seen. Once you're out of danger, ditch the car and move on by foot or in a different car.

SURVIVE A TSUNAMI

Tsunamis are large series of waves caused by earthquakes or volcanic eruptions on the ocean floor. They can travel for long distances and can be as tall as ten-story buildings, surging miles inland and crushing entire towns. There are more tsunamis in the Pacific Ocean than anywhere else in the world although they can happen in any ocean. The island nation of Japan suffers from the highest number of tsunamis, averaging about one every six or seven years.

In many parts of the world there are tsunami early-warning systems that will alert coastal residents if a deadly wave is on the way. But not always. The best way to survive a tsunami is to recognise the natural signs that danger is on the way. Then get to higher ground and get there fast.

WHAT TO DO

- ✓ If you're in a coastal area and you experience an earthquake, that may mean a tsunami is coming. Don't wait to find out.
- ✓ Tsunamis cause ocean water to recede dramatically. If you see the water rush out, get moving to higher ground.
- ✓ Hills, tall buildings or simply being far inland will improve your chances. Climb a tall strong tree as a last resort. Small trees can snap under the weight of all that water rushing in.
- ✓ Remember that tsunamis are a series of waves and that the second wave will likely be bigger and stronger than the first.
- ✓ If you do get swept up in the water, find something that floats and hold onto it. A tsunami will rush quickly back out to sea. Do not try to fight the current as that will only exhaust your strength. Your only hope is to ride it out and wait for rescuers to find you.

SURVIVE A PLANE CRASH

Most of the time, heroes can put their mettle and good sense to the test when it comes to survival. But not when it comes to surviving plane crashes. Tough as it is for any man to accept, luck more than knowledge is what you need on your side when the passenger jet you're on loses an engine in mid-air. That said, plane crashes don't happen very often – one statistic says the chances of getting into a plane crash are nine million to one. And even when planes do crash, there is a 95 per cent survival rate. Not bad chances, though they are chances nonetheless. To increase your luck there are a few things you can do before you get on that bucket of bolts and a few more things to try if the metal bird you're on does happen to go in for an emergency landing.

WHAT TO DO

1. Before you get on the plane, dress for success – success in a plane crash that is. If you go down – and you manage to survive – there's likely to be fire and you're going to need to move quickly without getting loose clothing caught on anything. Wear jeans, a long-sleeve cotton shirt, and lace-up shoes so that any burning debris falling on you will be less likely to land on skin. Avoid polyester, fleece or any other clothing that is flammable. Once you get out of the plane, it may also be cold so you'll need to stay warm. Carry a jacket on your lap, just in case.

2. Always reserve aisle seats at or near the exit. If you live through the crash, getting out of the plane is the key to survival. If you can't get close to the exit, try to book aisle seats close to the tail. One statistic says that passengers in the rear of the airplane are 40 per cent more likely to survive a crash than passengers near the front.

3. Once you're on the plane, read the safety card and listen to the flight attendant's safety speech – yes, yes, you've heard it all before but listen anyway. There's good information in there. Also, make a mental note of the nearest exits and how you plan to get to them. Count the aisles between you and the exits so you can get to them if it's totally dark.

4. Wear your seatbelt and keep it snug around your waist. Every centimetre of slack in your seatbelt triples the G-forces exerted on your body.

5. If you know you're going down, put on a lifejacket (if you're over water) or grab onto a jacket or blanket (if you're over mountains).

6. Brace yourself by putting your seat back up and placing your hands, one over the other, on the back of the seat in front of you. Your feet should move forward (broken legs are common in plane crashes because passengers put their feet under their seats).

7. After impact, unfasten your seatbelt and make your way as quickly as possible to the exits. Don't carry anything with you save for a jacket. Stay low, especially if there is smoke. Stay strong because there will be people panicking and trying to push over you. Don't let them. Stay orderly and listen to the flight attendants' instructions. If there is smoke, use a wet cloth to cover your mouth and nose to make breathing easier.

8. Once outside the plane, move quickly away from it. Most airlines say you should stay downwind about 150 m (500 ft) away in case the plane explodes.

9. If you end up in the water, remove shoes and excess clothing to make it easier to swim. Get as far away from the wreckage as possible, but stay within sight so that rescuers can find you easily.

CHAPTER

7

SUPERHERO STATUS

Now that we've covered the basics, it's time to put aside the novice work and learn how to ascend to a heroic level usually reserved for guys in capes and body stockings – that of the superhero. Of course, we won't be burning holes through iron bars with our laser vision or flying around the world at super sonic speeds – that requires a bigger book. We will, however, cover feats that most humans could (and possibly should) never do. Strap on your coloured underwear boys. It's time to man up and save the day.

JUMP A RAMP IN A CAR

The hero business and the stunt man business have many crossover points, one being doing ramp to ramp car jumps. In fact it is no coincidence that most heroes go on to successful careers in the movie industry and not a few stunt men have had their real-life heroic moments. And if you think jumping a car is impractical, think again. Almost every time you're in a car chase behind enemy lines with secret codes at stake, you'll need to know how to jump over the border security check point or leap over a river gorge in your getaway car.

WHAT TO DO

1. To jump a ramp in a car you have to know a little physics. How far you jump is going to depend on how heavy your car is, how fast you're going and the angle of the ramp. It's impossible to get far without a ramp so if you are behind enemy lines and you need to clear any security checkpoints, set up a ramp ahead of time.

2. With a ramp set up at a 45 degree angle you can't go too fast or the front end will bottom out on the ramp and you won't make your destination. You can fix this by lengthening the ramp.

3. You'll need to get up a speed of about 65 km (40 miles) per hour to clear roughly 7 m (25 ft), so be sure you have enough room to get to that speed.

4. When you hit the ramp, make sure your two front wheels hit the ramp at the same time. Otherwise, you'll go off the ramp sideways.

5. It's best to have a landing jump on the other side. Otherwise you'll come down hard, which could break your back, among other things. Ideally, you want to be coming down at the same angle as the ramp so the landing is smooth.

6. Also, give yourself plenty of room on the other side so you can have time to get the car under control and come to a stop.

DOS AND DON'TS

✓ Do practice. This is not one of those things you can just pick up as you go along. This will not work by closing your eyes, hitting the accelerator and praying. You want to know exactly what you're doing, so if you do foresee needing to jump a ramp, practice lots beforehand.

✗ Don't be over-ambitious. Start off with small distances and as you grow in confidence and skill, move on to more challenging jumps.

DRIVE A BUS AT HIGH SPEED

It may seem an unlikely scenario but a real hero is prepared for any situation. Being able to drive at high speed in a regular car is simple; doing the same in a big unwieldy bus is a whole other matter. It is larger, harder to handle, and more unstable. And you must be able to do so with a steady nerve, as you will be responsible for the safety of 50 other passengers as well as your own.

WHAT TO DO

1. Know your vehicle. There are a few fundamental differences between cars and buses. Apart from the obvious size and weight issues, buses are usually diesel, require double-clutch gear shifting and have powerful pneumatic brakes.

2. Due to a high centre of gravity, the bus will roll if you barrel into corners at high speed. The first signs of a roll will be from the back of the bus so as the driver, you may be unaware of the situation until it is too late. Listen for telltale screams from the back seats and respond appropriately.

3. If your runaway bus is lucky enough to have breaks, then keep checking the pressures are satisfactory, this is usually marked as green on the pressure gauge. Never pump the breaks as pressure will be lost and the breaks will lock and the bus will stop suddenly, due to its inbuilt safety device.

DOS AND DON'TS

✗ Do not drive through city areas or near schools in your speeding bus, keep to highways or perhaps a runway.

DIVE THROUGH A WINDOW

If you're trying to disarm a bomb and it's not going well, there may be a need for a last second escape. One hasty retreat is the old window dive. Just make sure of two things: the window you're diving out of is on the first floor and that it's open. Should neither be the case, and there's no other way out, try harder to diffuse the bomb.

You will need

large window (preferably on the ground floor)

courage

HOW TO

1. Make sure you get a good running start and push off with your legs. You want to be horizontal to the ground, but you also want your body to be at a slight angle.
2. As you go through the window, tuck your head down to avoid hitting it on anything above. Once you've made it through, you want to land in a judo roll.
3. Meet the ground with your hands first. They should be shoulder width apart and use your arm muscles to slow your fall.
4. After your hands hit the ground, tuck your head under so that the back of one shoulder hits the ground next, (that's why you dive at a slight angle, otherwise you would land on your neck) and roll your body and legs over into a standing position.
5. If done correctly the dive roll won't impede your escape at all. You should roll out into a full run.

SNATCH A CHILD FROM ONCOMING TRAFFIC

Most hero situations require quick thinking or more accurately no thinking at all: just action. If you see a child run out into the street to fetch a ball right in the pathway of an oncoming car you have seconds to act on your natural instincts. If you stop to think things through, it will all be tragically over before you have a chance to fling yourself heroically into the path of the oncoming car.

WHAT TO DO

1. Run fast towards the child.
2. While you're running at the child focus your eyes on their chest or back and get your arm out. You're going to scoop them up by placing one arm around their chest or back and under each armpit.
3. Don't stop when you reach the child. Just put your arm out like a hook, grab them and lunge out of the way.
4. In dire situations you may have to push a child out of the way and take the hit yourself. This is obviously not an ideal situation but you'll have a better chance of surviving getting hit by a car than a child would. A true hero is not going to let a car hit a child if he can help it.
5. If you are going to get hit by a car try to jump slightly before it reaches you so that you roll up on top of the hood into the windshield. Otherwise you'll get hit by the bumper and end up under the car where your chances of survival will not be good.

INTERVENE IN A MUGGING

Heroes are called upon to do all sorts of questionable things that mere mortals should never try. Some say stopping a mugging is one of those things. There are endless stories of people trying to intervene in a mugging and getting themselves shot. But this is hero time and if we see some thug trying to take advantage of a fair lady, then it's our duty to step in. Just don't get hasty and put yourself and that fair lady into a worse situation.

WHAT TO DO

1. If you see a mugging in progress, (you might see a struggle, witness someone pointing a gun at someone or hear someone scream 'stop him' or 'help!') always call the emergency services if you have time.
2. Then try yelling at the mugger something like 'hey, stop!' or 'I'm calling the police!' If a mugger knows someone is on to them many times they'll stop and run away.
3. If you're fairly sure you don't see a knife or gun, you could try yelling and running towards the mugger. This too will intimidate them into abandoning their mugging.
4. Purse snatchers will try to grab and run. If one runs by you, stick your foot out to trip them, give them a blast of pepper spray as they pass or lower a shoulder into their body to knock them down. Often if a mugger is surprised like that they'll leave the purse and run. You could try to pin the mugger to the ground and make them give up the goods or hold them until the police arrive but you need to be sure you have the strength to do that.
5. Lastly, take a good look at the mugger and report what you've seen to the police.

CONTROL A RUNAWAY HORSE

If adventure is your middle name you may run across a few emergencies that have nothing to do with natural disaster. Those working with horses or as movie stuntmen attached to epic Sergio Leoni-style westerns may in fact be moved to action while atop a runaway horse.

If this happens to you, just know that horses are large, powerful animals, but they're often cowards at heart. That's because they have a long history of being a prey animal and their natural response to sudden movement or loud noise is to take off running first and ask questions later. They scare easily.

WHAT TO DO

1. First, stay calm. If a runaway horse has a scared, screaming human on his back it's going to make him run faster.
2. Make sure you're not the problem. Don't dig your heels into the horse's side. Flapping arms and clothes may also excite the horse.
3. Steer the horse into a clearing, lean forward and grab hold of one rein as close to the bit as possible.
4. Pull up on the rein and sit up at the same time. This will cause the horse's head to turn to one side and he will begin to run in a circle. Make sure you've given the rein enough slack on the opposite side you're pulling on.
5. The idea is that if you keep the horse going in a circle he will tire of running and will soon calm down enough to respond to his normal signal for 'stop' or 'whoa' or whatever you say to get a horse to stand still.

If you find yourself riding a runaway horse, one option is to focus on riding him rather than trying to stop him. To do this, focus on maintaining your balance while simultaneously loosening your muscles – tight muscles will enhance the bounce of the horse. Also, keep your body upright to prevent yourself from going over the horse's shoulder if he makes a sudden turn or stop. You will eventually be able to control the horse again, so just control your mind, don't panic, and get into the rhythm of the ride until the horse calms down.

If riding it out doesn't work, another option is to employ an emergency stop. If you're headed towards heavy traffic, low branches or any other dangerous situation then this might be your only option. Emergency stops don't work for all riders, in all situations, or with all horses and their effectiveness will depend on your skill level and the horse's training.

HOW TO FEND OFF WILD ANIMALS

Should your heroic actions take you into the wilderness, you may find a different kind of threat: wild animals. They won't be carrying guns and knives – only teeth, claws and a ferocious animal instinct that's far more scary than any wimpy mugger or house robber. Here are some suggestions on how to deal with a few of the wilder animals in the jungle.

BEARS

Unless they are surprised or protecting their cubs, bears aren't usually aggressive toward humans. If you run across a black bear back slowly away from it, waving your hands, yelling or blowing a whistle. Usually it will wander off. Waving at and jumping up and down in front of a grizzly bear, however, will do the exact opposite. In this case your only hope may be to lie down, play dead and pray it leaves you alone.

BIG CATS

If you happen to stumble into a big cat, the worst thing you can do is turn around and run. Cats always pounce on and attack their victims from behind. It's better to turn and face the cat and start waving your hands, yelling or blowing a whistle.

CROCODILES

Often mistaken for floating logs until it's too late, a tangle with a crocodile can faze even the most heroic adventurer. The best thing to do is avoid their hangouts if you can – thirsty-looking wildebeest and one-armed locals are classic giveaways. If you do spot a crocodile bearing down on you, play dead and hope it passes you by, looking for a livelier meal.

ELEPHANTS

Unless you're in Africa or India, you are unlikely to stumble into an elephant or two while on a casual outing. But if you do, and the beast starts charging after you, the best option is to stand absolutely still. Most elephant charges are bluffs and if they can see that you're not impressed with their size, flapping ears and loud snorts then they'll go back to pruning the surrounding trees.

SHARKS

Sharks often approach from below in an attempt to break their prey in two with one bite – a fate to be avoided where possible. This also means you're unlikely to see that infamous triangular fin approach. Stay aware of other swimmers disappearing and the warnings of the lifeguard, if there is one. It's also wise to stay out of the water if you have an open wound – a sharks' ability to sniff out blood is legendary.

SNAKES

Most snakebites occur when humans stumble on a snake and startle it. The best way to prevent this is to be cautious when walking around and sitting on logs in areas with high snake populations.

TIP

If you do get bitten by a snake do not cut open the wound with a knife. Simply suck a shallow wound for about five minutes, spitting out the venom. If it appears to be a deeper bite, keep the wound below your heart, loosen any constrictive clothing and get yourself to a hospital.

TALK DOWN A SUICIDAL JUMPER

Let's say you're walking down the street and you see high above the crowds a person standing on the ledge of a 12-story building. You might assume that this is another superhero in the making and he's about to test out his flying skills. But then you might remember that people don't actually have the ability to fly, which would lead you to another conclusion: they're going to jump! The real superhero at this point needs to be you.

WHAT TO DO

1. The first step is to stay calm and call emergency services. If you can leave it to a trained expert, you should always do so. Only get involved when you really have no other option. In which case you should slowly approach the jumper and start talking.
2. You need to establish yourself as an authority figure who can help them. You might think that the suicidal person needs a friend to talk to but research has shown that if you try to befriend the jumper they'll jump anyway. You need to let them know that it's not okay to jump.
3. As you're talking to a jumper move closer to them, inch by inch, but carefully. You don't want to crowd a jumper quickly but if you can get close to them while talking then you can grab them if you need to.
4. During the conversation, don't think that you can turn a person's life around and suddenly make them happy if they're depressed. It won't happen. They need help and you're there to help them get it.
5. Also, because of the aforementioned reason, don't trust a jumper. If he or she says, 'I'm feeling much better', don't believe them. Keep talking about getting help and how it's not okay to just kill yourself.

HOW TO CATCH A THIEF

If you've been burgled, then you know you don't want it to happen again. Not only do you loose your stuff but you feel violated. It's a challenge to your manhood. Someone sneaked into your home and took your things and all you can do is picture them with a big smile on their face and a big stamp on your forehead that says 'sucker'. Next time you'll be ready.

WHAT TO DO

1. Preventing a burglary is a much better course of action than having to deal with a thief. Make sure all your doors and windows are locked. It sounds obvious, but some experts say that most burglaries happen because the thief can get in easily. Also, don't leave ladders or outdoor tables in the front garden – that gives people tools to climb to the second story.
2. Install a home alarm system, ideally one that alerts the local police department when you're out of town. If you're really paranoid, set up a home surveillance system with web-cams. Of course, if you still find a thief in the house then trying to catch them is the next step.
3. The first thing you need is the element of surprise. Without that things will be much harder.
4. Always call the emergency services first as long as it's not going to give you away. If you think you can't catch the thief, get away from the scene as fast and quietly as possible and then call the police.
5. If the robbery is taking place in your house, just remember that you know its layout far better than the thief does. Use it to your advantage. Get frying pans, kitchen knives or anything else you have to defend yourself and render the thief unconscious.

HOW TO DODGE A BULLET

If you find yourself in a hostile situation staring down the barrel of a gun, the ideal course of action would be to do as you are told, or try to disarm the gunman. Of course that is much easier said than done, and if faced with a trigger-happy gunman, you may find it necessary to 'dodge' a bullet. Of course, as you sadly don't have the speed or reactions of a superhero, there will be no real dodging at all. You can however, try to anticipate a shot, and then try to get behind something or run away.

WHAT TO DO

1. To anticipate a shot you have to be highly observant. Take note of the gun wielder's attitude. Is he getting impatient, angry or scared? All these things may mean he'll take a shot soon. Also, take a close look at his trigger finger and where he is aiming the gun. If his hand is loose and relaxed you may be fine. If his knuckles are white then he might be ready to pull the trigger. To dodge a bullet, your goal is to move faster than his trigger finger.

2. If you sense a shot is coming push off with one leg and move quickly either left or right, depending on which hand the gunman is holding his gun in. If the gun is in his right hand, move left. Vice versa for a lefty gunman. That's because it's slightly harder to move across the body with a gun and be accurate with a shot.

3. If you successfully dodge the first shot, don't stop there. Run for cover, preferably big cover. Like a building. Once you get behind something keep that thing between you and the gunman.

4. If you have to run away from an assailant in an open place, run in a zigzag, erratic route so he has trouble taking aim at you.

JUMP FROM A PLANE

Let's say you're high in the air battling bad guys. You've overpowered them all, but during the struggle, someone landed on the control panels and destroyed all chances of you trying to land the plane safely. You're going to have to strap on a parachute and jump. If you can't find a parachute, skip this section and go back to 'Surviving a Plane Crash' on page 106.

WHAT TO DO

1. Grab a parachute, and look for a 'handle' near the bottom of the pack that is attached to a pin fitted into a silver grommet. This is what you're going to pull to release the chute.
2. Put the chute on. It fits like a cross between a climbing harness (over your legs and around your waist) and a backpack (with shoulder straps). Reach around to your lower back and familiarise yourself with where the release handle is located – this will be important later.
3. Make sure the plane is at a low altitude and is slowing down. If you're above 5 km (16,000 ft) you'll need an oxygen tank to breathe on the way down.
4. When the time is right, move to the back of the plane, open the door, and jump. Keep up a stable freefall position.
5. Count to ten, then reach around to your lower back and pull the release handle to deploy the chute.
6. If it doesn't, you need to pull the rings on the front of your shoulder straps out at the same time and the backup chute will automatically deploy.

FOIL A BANK ROBBERY

Truly any man with aspirations of heroism would welcome a good bank robbery just so he could foil it. The problem is there's no one way to do it. You don't know if you'll be in the bank or walking past one when it happens. You could be driving when the robbers take off or perhaps you've overheard some guys plotting the robbery before it ever happens. In any situation you'll have to think on your feet – fast – and adjust your foiling tactics accordingly.

Of course, as in any situation involving guns and angry robbers, the most heroic thing you probably should do is nothing. Sometimes a man trying to be a 'hero' ends up putting himself and the others around him in more danger. Don't do that. Instead be smart and try to retain the element of surprise.

WHAT TO DO

1. Often bank robbers don't charge into banks with guns blazing. Most of the time, they come in and walk up to a bank teller. These types often have hats and sunglasses on and wear long coats. If you see someone like this, don't take any chances, alert a security guard.

2. If you work at a bank and someone like this comes up to you, don't wait to hear what he or she has to say. Simply act as nice as you can, let them know you haven't seen them in the bank before and ask them to follow you over to a 'new account' manager. Then ask them subtly to remove their hat and sunglasses and present an ID so you can get started. Usually, robbers will be flustered at this kindness and they'll leave.

3. Sometimes team work is the best way to foil a robbery. No one likes the idea of some guy coming in and stealing their hard work, so try and enlist the support of others in the bank. If you can disarm the gunman or wrestle him to the ground, start calling out instructions such as 'someone call the police!' or 'get the gun!' or 'get him off of me!' There's a good chance that if you physically engage the robber, others are going to discover their inner hero as well and help you out.
4. If you're outside and a masked man runs out with a bag, try to trip him or lower a shoulder. Review the 'how to stop a mugger' section.
5. Another effective technique is the grab bag. If you can grab the money bag and run or rip it open so that the cash spills out, most of the time the robber will take off.
6. If you're in a car and the robbers are trying to drive or run away, use your car to ram them. Don't worry, the police probably won't issue you a ticket if you've helped catch a robber.

REAL-LIFE HERO

To be a real-life hero, you don't have to build a secret headquarters in your basement, become a misunderstood vigilante or even buy a cape with a logo. As you have seen, heroism comes in all forms and it is needed everyday in all manner of situations, from the subtle acts of romance toward the lady in your life to the more ostentatious crash landing of a plane or dodging a bullet. It is true that danger may not lurk around every corner, but you never know when or where it will appear. When it does, people will need a hero, and in these darkest times of need, you'll be ready. You can bravely step forward, with a steely look and determined step, and heroically save the day.

INDEX